BANNED IN BRITAIN

BEATING THE LIBERAL
BLACKLIST

BANNED IN
BRITAIN

BEATING THE LIBERAL
BLACKLIST

First Edition
First Printing

MICHAEL
SAVAGE

SPI
SAVAGE
PRODUCTIONS INC.

www.michaelsavage.com

First Edition, First Printing, October 2009

Published in Kissimmee, FL by Savage Productions, Inc.
c/o Marlin Logistics
3600 Commerce Blvd
Kissimmee, FL 34741

ISBN Number 978-1-4276-4253-0

Printed in the United States of America

09 10 11 12 13   5 4 3 2 1

*Dedicated to all the men who died
defending freedom of speech*

Table of Contents

Table of Contents

Foreword

Foreword

The Speech That Never Was:
Cancelled by Government Intimidation
by Dr. Michael Savage
for the Cambridge Union Debate
Originally Scheduled for October 15, 2009

M r. President, my fellow debaters, ladies and gentlemen:

I have been invited to debate before you tonight against the insanity of political correctness because a terrible injustice has been done. In May of this year, former Home Secretary Jacqui Smith released a list of murderers and terrorists banned from entering the United Kingdom. My name was also included on this list. In doing so, she has linked and listed one of America's most beloved radio talk show hosts—with 10 million listeners—alongside Russian skinheads in prison for murdering 10 immigrants and a Hamas murderer who executed two Jewish parents and crushed the head of their four-year-old daughter. Would not criminals of this caliber be arrested immediately upon entry into the United Kingdom, or does this imply that all but those on the list are allowed? Osama bin Laden was not on this list, is he allowed to enter the United Kingdom?

Why would someone who has never committed a crime, nor appeared as a defendant in a criminal trial, nor been accused of an actual crime be placed on such a high profile list by a major player in international politics? I say that it is because of the continuing erosion of freedom of speech in America, in the United

Kingdom, and in all nations where such liberties are supposedly granted, and this under the dirty veil of political correctness. My continued dedication to the principles of borders, language and culture should seem no threat to a nation diligently aware of its national identity. Admittedly, in my broadcasts I may not reflect the keen and cool dignity of British gentility, but I have Saville Row in my soul.

I must assume, then, that I pose a threat to the government, and one just as frightening as the most dangerous of international terrors–the thought criminal. This is a person whose thoughts and ideas are so powerful that they lead people to disobey the establishment. George Washington, whose mother was a Tory, knew when his countrymen were being unfairly taxed, used, and persecuted. This made him a thought criminal of England. History has shown us that when injustice is being done to a people, they rebel. It is the quiet, 'peaceful' decisions made behind closed doors and seedy backroom policies shrouded in smoke that provoke the people. Secret decisions with no oversight or communication are the kind which sidestep laws and civil liberties, with total disregard for the voting public. This is what led to the tyrants Hitler, Stalin, Castro and Hugo Chavez: Rulers, when given an inch will run thousands of miles, perhaps right through our own homes.

People who disagree with the *status quo* must speak up and be counted for, speak for themselves, and question authority. I have done nothing but this, yet my opinions are casually shrugged off by liberals in the government andin the media as valueless because they are not 'politically correct', an ideology with strict guidelines for what should be said and what should not be said in the limelight. As political correctness erodes the volume and value of our vocabulary, so too does it erode our freedom of speech and freedom to hold our lawmakers accountable, an idea which in a modern sense can be traced at least as far back as the Magna Carta. People and their culture are not to be homogenized until they are compatible with other cultures and people; compatibility must come from within, from debate and discourse and compromise, and even legislation. Not from an arbitrary standard which might work for some people in some cases, but not as Lincoln said, for "all of the people all of the time."

What kind of kingdom has Britain become? Isn't free speech a value that Western nations must preserve at all costs, one which sets us apart from dictatorship, anarchy, and fatal corruption? Yet it is precisely because of my freedom of speech that I have been targeted by the socialist government in England. This, combined with the appointment of Mark Lloyd as the FCC's new 'Diversity Czar' in the United States is just another step towards the extinguishing of independent thought on the airwaves and the 'restructuring' of free media based on Lloyd's diatribe 'The Structural Imbalance of Political Talk Radio'. In 2007, I was awarded the Freedom of Speech Award by *Talker Magazine*. How could the winner of such an award be singled out and banned from traveling to Britain?

I remember the 1960s when true liberals used to say, "I may disagree with you but I would fight to the death your right to say it." When have you last heard a liberal say, "Oh I may disagree with conservative talk radio, but I would fight to the death their right to say what they believe in"? I don't hear that anymore. What instead I hear is, "I think it's time to pass a standard...to bring accountability to the airwaves." That was stated earlier this year by left wing Democrats in the U.S. House of Representatives. Is that liberalism?

Aren't Britain and the U.S. about freedom of speech? That's what this country has been about from the day it was founded. That's the trail of tears and the trail of blood that led to the freedoms that we enjoy in this country today, and we cannot permit a few small minded martinets who don't even know they're inhabiting the souls of dictatorships in Congress right now to deny us our freedom of speech. Where are the true good liberals?

Radio is in a more perilous state today than it's been in its entire history. In South America, the dictator Hugo Chavez closed down the opposition media in Venezuela. You might say, "Well that can't happen here." It can happen in America. As I speak with you it *is* happening in America. Senator Tom Harkin of Iowa, Senator Jeff Bingaman of New Mexico, Senator Richard Durbin of Illinois and even House Speaker Nancy Pelosi were recently circulating a bill in Congress for the so-called "Fairness Doctrine." This bill would require the holders of broadcast licenses to present controversial issues of public importance in a manner that was (in the view of the Federal Communications Commission) honest, equitable and balanced.

This is a form of political 'correctness'. What this means is people such as myself will no longer be able to speak freely. Is that any different than Chavez closing down opposition media? Is that not dictatorship, the Fairness Doctrine? Of course it is. It's just that we use fancy rhetoric in this country as opposed to police power. But make no mistake about it: The Fairness Doctrine is political correctness. It is censorship, and it has no place in the United States of America.

Now let me give you some examples, if I may, about the power of freedom of speech in talk radio:

Al Gore, for example, in my opinion, lies when he preaches that all scientists now agree that global warming is caused by human activity. If I refute Gore's lies on the airwaves by quoting numerous prominent scientists who refute Gore's hysterical con, I am using freedom of speech granted to us by the United States Constitution to do so. If radical environmental folks were to make it a crime to deny global warming–*aha!*–You've heard that! They say they want to make it a crime to deny global warming. Such refutations as mine and those of prominent scientists would be banished from the discussion.

Ahmadinejad, the new Hitler of our time, the so-called President of Iran, has declared his desire to create a new holocaust against the Jews. And yet we see prominent lawyers and journalists, some of Jewish descent, in our own country, denying the Islamo-fascist connection. Worse, even defending Islamic murderers, for example, in Guantanamo, who would gladly cut their throats and decapitate them while chanting to Allah. Out of fear of offending the SS of today, they refuse to talk about the codification of hatred for Jews, Israel, the United States, and our way of life. That's freedom of speech, is it not? Well, what is freedom of speech? Why do these intellectuals deny their own freedom of speech to defend the freedom to preach hatred by their enemies?

I want to define satire, ridicule and sarcasm. *Satire* is the use of irony, sarcasm, ridicule, or the like in exposing, denouncing, or deriding vice, folly, etc. What is *ridicule?* We use it on talk radio all the time if we know how. It is speech or action intended to cause contemptuous laughter at a person or thing. Derision, derision, my friends, is ridicule. That's part of freedom of speech. And finally, sarcasm should be used all the time if you know how to do it. What is *sarcasm?* It's harsh or bitter derision or irony; a sharply ironical taunt; a sneering or cutting remark, a review full of sarcasms. That's freedom of speech, sure to offend those targeted!

When I offend doctrinaire, knee-jerk Republicans–yes, I don't limit my criticism to the Democrats or the liberals–by pointing out the contractor abuses in Iraq and in Afghanistan, whose freedoms am I denying? The freedoms of the military/industrial complex to rob the public? Eisenhower warned us, "Beware the military-industrial complex." I've played that on my show over and over again. Who am I criticizing, Democrats or Republicans? I'll let you decide.

When I state that our Army and Marine heroes are being sent in to fight door to door and suffer and die–suffer and die–and then be given court-martials if they do their job a little too well, because Obama is either the most hesitant or incompetent Commander in Chief in the United States' history, whose freedoms am I denying? President Bush said he would not have politicians telling our generals how to conduct the war. Well, I wonder, was he not a politician, telling generals how to conduct the war? No war had ever been conducted like this. The same is being repeated by President Obama in Afghanistan.

When I call illegal aliens 'invaders' and I present the social and fiscal drain of this invading army of illegal aliens, whose freedoms am I denying? Who am I offending? Is it the doctrinaire, knee-jerk Republicans, or the Democrats? Probably both.

When I, Michael Savage, support my position for borders, language and culture, do I deny my fellow citizens their rights to redress their grievances to a government all too eager to continue flooding our nation with cheap laborers? When I present the fact that 30%, or one of three prisoners in federal prison is an illegal alien who doesn't belong here to begin with, do I deny, or do I grant my fellow U.S. citizens their right to speak freely through me, a talk show host? Whose rights am I offending? Certain special interests, I would assume.

If these and other like opinions of mine were mine alone, I would not have risen to this position I now enjoy in the world of the spoken and written word. In fact, I am the voice of the voiceless who have been marginalized and silenced by the illiberal liberals who control virtually–virtually–all avenues of images and ideas that the world sees. All images and ideas with the limited exception of conservative talk radio, the most vulnerable medium now under attack by the new National Socialists who would ban free speech that they disagree with by threatening corporate sponsors through extortionist means of false boycotts, by using different techniques, but wanting to achieve the same ends of all dictatorships. That is total control of speech which is the opposite of freedom of speech. Not only is this politically incorrect, it is categorically incorrect. So-called 'political correctness' has no place in a free society. Remember this: The first amendment to the U.S. Constitution was not written to protect politespeech.

It was written to protect offensive speech. Vigorous, loud debate is the hallmark of a free society, not the pitiful morgue of politeness.

Preface

Preface

The Savage Fight Against Censorship

*'Tis the Majority
In this, as All, prevail–
Assent, and you are sane–
Demur, you're straightway dangerous–
And handled with a Chain–*

-Emily Dickinson (1830-1886)

I've led somewhat of a life of charm until now, with a few bumps…until now. I finally hit a stone wall–the old, cracked but never breaking stone walls of monarchic England. Our original oppressive ruler. Now quasi-Marxist do-gooders, fearing for their lives, pick on the innocent to protect the liberty of the guilty.

Overrun by the insanity of their own policies of ultra-tolerance, they choose intolerance as a quick defense. The once-proud British of Churchill, the victors of the Battle of Britain where so many flowers of Cambridge and Oxford nobly sacrificed their lives–now reduced to broken flower pots of people ruling Britannia. Overrun by people who hate them. Hate their race. Hate their Whiteness. The broken shards of England choose to condemn an American Patriot. A man who speaks of borders, of language, of culture. He is the enemy of the shards of England's pride. He is now the sum total of all that threatens the island's survival.

This free spirit ensnared by the descendents of those bold Norsemen now fallen. Their clay feet crumbling.

Although the news story in blaring headlines was that Michael Savage, talk show host, was banned in Britain, the subtext was really:

"Michael Savage, nationalist and patriot, banned from the globalist system."

The rationalization provided for the ban was nothing more than a collection of sound-bites taken out of context. They were used to put me in league with murderers and terrorists in order to castigate me and make me appear to be a genuinely bad guy. The fact of the matter is that this is a subterfuge by globalist power-players to make sure that any true nationalist, even a non-violent nationalist, is criminalized.

In this book, I will reveal my never-ending quest for free speech in Britain and here in the United States. I have the right to speak freely according to both US law and even British law, without being libeled and censored. I will explain how I've been attacked because I have attempted to define America–and, for that matter, all nations–by their borders, language, and culture.

Those three concepts of *borders* and *language* and *culture* are anathema to the architects of the new globalist system. They believe there should be no borders, no single language, and certainly no culture. There should only be a world without borders, a polyglot of languages, and a culture built upon no culture. In the place of culture, they want consumerism. In place of government of the people, by the people, and for the people, they want government of the bureaucrats, by the bureaucrats, and for the bureaucrats.

So they want me silenced.

Forever.

Gone.

Without another word.

Whether you agree with nationalism or not, do you really want an international order where political rulers are free to destroy people who disagree with them?

In a sense, they have "made" me the enemy of the New World Order. In this book, I describe the punishment the British government has inflicted upon me for saying things that they disagree with. I also explain why I speak out as I do, even though it makes me a target. I carefully detail the attack upon the West, using radical Islam as a tool by the New World Order communists. Let us not forget that it has long been a dream of communists to dominate the world with worldwide socialism. Now that we clearly have a neo-Marxist as president who has moved faster towards socialism in America than FDR did in the first four years of his administration, it becomes abundantly clear that we must protest more loudly than ever against this knife that is aimed at our throats.

While this is a book where I voice many of my conservative opinions, it is not just a book only for conservatives, but for any man or woman who cares about free speech. This is a book for anyone who believes that the government should not censor speech nor use their power to intimidate people from speaking out freely.

This is a book for true liberals as well as conservatives—whether you're a Democrat, a Republican, a Libertarian or an Independent.

Make no mistake about it; you will not be freer under a globalist regime, or free at all. You will not have more liberty in a globalist regime. You will be living under the yoke of a nameless, faithless bureaucracy—probably headquartered somewhere in Europe.

Have "Borders, Language, Culture" Become Illegal?

One of the most challenging aspects of writing this book was the constantly changing information. Relevant news would break every week, if not every day. As I write this, for example, I get to read about how a terrorist killer gets "humanitarian" treatment, by being allowed to go home to a hero's welcome. The British government that added my name to a "ban" list—the very same group!—released the Libyan terrorist who was convicted of blowing up Pan American Flight #103 killing 270 people! The Libyan went home to a hero's welcome (why not give the guy a parade?) while I, Michael Savage, was left to suffer in silence.

It is the height of insanity that as I fight to have my name taken off a banned list of murderers and terrorists, another murderer and terrorist, Abdel Baset al-Megrahi, the madman responsible for the Lockerbie bombing and the deaths of over 200 people, is being released by the British government. The government claims that it is doing so on humanitarian grounds because he is sick. Did Megrahi consider humanitarian interest as the bomb which ripped apart the lives of hundreds of families was exploding over the skies of Scotland? It gets worse when you consider the footage of him getting on and off the plane. In Scotland, they were shaking his hand as he boarded! And when he de-planed in Libya, he was greeted by waving flags and a hero's welcome–for this scum of the earth! The British government is suicidal. They have sympathy for those who kill their people and antipathy for those that defend them!

Of course, when I first heard of this horror, I thought there was probably real economic pressure behind this decision. Gordon Brown actually traveled to Saudi Arabia when the financial crisis hit in order to get help.[1] It is open knowledge that the Labour government and the British Crown will do nothing to offend the Saudi King because of their need for Saudi oil and for Saudi purchase of British arms.[2] The vow to never offend Islam is so strong that a member of parliament can get into serious trouble simply for choosing not to remain at a wedding party because it was segregated, separating men and women.[3] This is the crux of the issue. I advocate that each country or nation preserve its borders, language, and culture. But speaking up for borders, language, and culture gets in the way of global governance.

I can only wonder why my website happened to get seriously hacked the same day that the news about the release of Megrahi was reported.[4]

The Prime Minister Gordon Brown cares less than I do about his nation's borders, language, and culture. It actually came out the next day that Libya's Gadaffi had been lobbying Britain for the bomber's release while in trade discussions with the British government. He said he continually negotiated for the bomber's release and referred to Brown as a "courageous friend," who had done what he requested.[5] Of course there were howls of denial, but then the *Sunday Times* in London broke the story, with the revealed documents, "Lockerbie Bomber 'Set Free for Oil.'"[6]

So, based on the secret emails and documents my team uncovered, the Prime Minister was in favor of banning and libeling me while he was negotiating with Libya for economic reasons–even pressuring Scotland to release the Lockerbie bomber. Nice.

Reading about this made me wonder for the first time if my name had ever come up in the Prime Minister's economic negotiations with Islamic nations.

As I just mentioned, one of the main turning points (that happened during the writing of the book) was the uncovering of secret government documents that dealt with the decision to ban me (more about this in chapter 1). In reading through the legal background on my being banned in England by this group of snot-nosed effete snobs, I was shocked by the clinical efficiency of their emails to each other. Their snickering little schoolboy emails to each other, filled with statements such as "I will hold down the fort" and things of that nature, revealed the sheer pettiness of the goals and short-sighted thinking of these officials.

But what most alarmed me was, when reading these emails where they were discussing whether or not to ban a radio talk show host from America by putting him on a list with terrorists and murderers and the ramifications thereof, I felt as though I was reading archival documents that were found somewhere in the Nazi era from Germany. In other words, archives of the Nazi era would have read just as clinically.

I could not believe how clinically they analyzed whether to ban me and what effect it might have, and whether to notify me. I could not believe how they had the nerve to say that they wouldn't notify me because they didn't know where I live. How could they not know where I live when they quote that I'm syndicated by Talk Radio Network in every other correspondence? How could they not know how to reach me when I have an audience of eight million? Moreover, they decided that they were "still not sure about naming him as this may create a following which he never had before."

They go on further and say that *if we do have any ramifications from banning an American broadcaster here's how we're going to cover our tracks. We must be careful to say the following....* Then they list their strategic plan in steps one, two, three. First, they plan to deny that they ever comment on individual cases, then that they have the authority necessary, and finally "Exclusion powers are very serious and no decision to exclude is taken lightly or as a method of stopping open debate on issues."

That's ridiculous because in every other statement they say that I advocate borders, language and culture as the definition of a nation. "What he claims to stand for are borders, language and culture, the three primary constituents of any nation as far as Savage is concerned." This belief, for which I stand, is brought up more than once. That's now a crime? It's now illegal to define a nation by its borders, language and culture?

Do you have any idea what this means? It means that the liberals have become the most extreme form of "thought police." It means that the liberals have declared conservatives criminal. It means that the liberals in England have criminalized conservative thought and conservative speech. Which is why every *real* liberal who really believes in the liberal Credo should read my book, *Banned in Britain*. You need it as a document. You need to see the proof. You need to see I'm not hyping you. And you need to share it with your liberal friends. It may finally awaken them from their slumber before it is too late. It just might save America from the fate that Britain is suffering under this Labour government.

I am one man fighting an entire government. Do you understand what is at stake? I hope you do. And I hope you understand that this is not hype. I do not care about selling a certain number of books because it will fatten my wallet. I hope you understand that I'm well past that point in my life. I hope you understand that there's a greater principle in this book about being banned in Britain: it is one man's fight to free his name from this list of murderers and terrorists.

Yes, what has happened is everything I warned my listeners about leftist governments and worse. They do not respect a nation's borders, language or culture; they do want to take apart your nation at the joints; they do want to flood you with illegal immigrants; they do want to polyglot your language; they do want to decimate your culture. Everything I have warned you about for 15 years has come out in these despicable emails.

Coming Attractions

The book begins with the battle story in chapter one, "Savage Strikes Back," providing details about my response to being banned from Britain, and the blows that have been traded since that time. I also defend myself from false accusations. My appeal to Hillary Clinton is detailed, as is my response to the British government's lies about me. This response involves the use of a British law firm, and I show how they have struggled on my behalf in letters to the Home Office. I also show that I began to do all I could to use the British media's curiosity about me to make my case, including giving interviews to the BBC.

In addition, the alleged "Sir" Nigel Sheinwald, the British Ambassador to the US, then perpetrated further damage against my name and reputation, and I responded. I discuss the partial victory won in pressuring Jacqui Smith to step down from her position, and my plans for further action to stop this insidious threat to free speech.

Chapter two details the events of May 5, 2009, recounting how I learned, to my amazement, that I had been publicly linked with killers and terrorists by an official decision and declaration by the British government. The authority behind this decision came from the highest offices in the British government–right up to Prime Minister Gordon Brown–according to secret government emails.

This chapter will briefly introduce the attackers and what they did to me and, in principle, to anyone who dares to speak in a way the government finds reprehensible. I show the hypocrisy of their ruling and emphasize the deficiencies in their character by contrasting Britain's current government to that of the great Winston Churchill.

While an attack on free speech is of concern to everyone, it is helpful to understand why I was particularly singled out. The next chapter goes into more detail, explaining how I am opposed to Globalism. Instead, I want to preserve America's borders, language, and culture. I also show how the anti-nation, anti-culture, open-borders agenda of globalism is bringing ruin to Britain and Europe. And it's also hurting the United States.

As I will reveal, the rise of globalism has come, by no coincidence, with a rise in opposition to free speech. Globalism requires censorship.

In chapter four, I turn from England to our own United States. The problem with the defamation spread by the British government is that it amounts to punishment of free speech or any words that the government doesn't like. One can have the legal freedom to speak one's mind, but be constrained by fear that the government will find some way to punish you. That is not free speech.

In this chapter I show how this pattern of intimidation is not restricted to the other side of the Atlantic. A pattern of hostility and intimidation has emerged through our own Department of Homeland Security. This chapter discusses the attack on conservatives published by a "Fusion Center" in Missouri. Then it turns to the national problem of the memo on "Rightwing Extremism," put out by the

Department of Homeland Security. In both of these two cases, Americans learned that, if they are conservative, they are being watched by Obama's henchwoman.

Having established that America is following in England's steps, chapter five returns to Britain's attack on me, highlighting how others have responded to this assault on liberty. I reveal how some true liberals supported me in accordance with basic civil libertarian principles. For example, I was treated quite fairly and objectively in a *New Yorker* magazine profile. On the other hand, my treatment by Fox News was Stalinist. Just as Stalin removed all evidence of the existence of some people, most of Fox News ignored the most important free speech case in the news rather than acknowledge my existence. I also discuss how listeners and loyal bloggers rallied to my support. Finally, I review my own faithfulness to my ideals in the face of this attack.

How did we get to this point? Chapter six explains our current dire situation, beginning with the rise of Obama to the Presidency. I then discuss the last days of George W. Bush and the legacy he left us, and how he prepared the way for Obama's neo-Marxist regime. The chapter ends with a sketch of The Era of Obama. I write about Obama's neo-Marxism as it has been applied to date, discussing his executive orders and his unprecedented number of "Czars."

Chapter seven continues to examine what has gone wrong in our country, especially singling out the bailout mania that is enabling the government to have unprecedented control over the private sector. The bailouts reveal a sordid tale of corruption in both parties in which the bailed-out companies financially supported both candidates and were then benefited by the politicians. Such financial power in the hands of politicians, along with such great financial corruption, gives politicians new tools and new reasons to intimidate free speech.

While free speech is important for its own sake, it is also important because conservatives need to speak out on important issues. Chapter eight deals with some of this dilemma. While it is not politically correct to say so, we continue to have threats to face abroad.

Islamo-fascists at home and abroad mean us harm while North Korea continues to grow as an unstable threat that has acquired nuclear capability. China also continues to grow as a rival and as an economic power. Furthermore, we must deal with South American dictators like Hugo Chavez. Chapter eight also looks at the home front and the problems of illegal immigration and Obama's plan for amnesty.

In the Epilogue, I conclude by presenting readers with an action plan for saving America from a complete takeover by Marxist-Leninist thugs. I also describe some things you can do to help me and help free speech in America.

I've included two Appendixes at the end of the book. The first is an enlightening interview I conducted with John O'Sullivan, the executive editor of Radio Free Europe/Radio Liberty in Prague, after he wrote a story about my situation in the *New York Post*. The second is a model for a Petition you can send to Congress for the removal of my name from Britain's list.

The New Yorker Magazine Profile

While writing this book, I was extremely encouraged by a profile written by Kelefa Sanneh about me that appeared in *The New Yorker*. While thankful for the publicity, which was positive without agreeing with my point of view (objective journalism is not quite dead yet, thankfully!), there was more about this profile that really helped me in my struggle.

The New Yorker profile confirmed that the Home Office's attack on me is not only about me. I have the odd and unique privilege to represent two important groups in America. I represent the battle for the freedom of conservative talk radio and conservatives across the nation, and also represent the right of any true independent to be left alone uncensored and uncoerced in modern society. The profile in *The New Yorker* captured these two aspects rather well.

The profile also confirmed that though liberals may disagree with me–and in many cases disagree with me as strongly as I do with them–they can (if they want to) distinguish between my saying something they disagree with and my calling for murder as the British Government falsely accused me. For example:

> The form of Savage's show–the quick cuts from one topic to another, the way familiar political observations give rise to baffling digressions, the fluctuating tension between his blue-state life and his red-state message–is at least as important as its content, which means that it's hard to understand him, and his appeal, at second hand.

> The immoderate quotes meticulously catalogued by the liberal
> media-watchdog site mediamatters.org are accurate but misleading,
> insofar as they reduce a willfully erratic broadcast to a series of polit-
> ical brickbats.[7]

This is exactly right, and it is encouraging that someone who is not ideologically aligned with me can see it.

I must add that, despite the importance of my fight with the British Home
Office and with the American government for free speech, *The New Yorker* profile is more important to me simply because it is an honor to be profiled by them.
I never suspected, as I grew up reading *The New Yorker*, that I would ever be profiled. It puts me in the league of giants.

A few of those who have been profiled in past years include Mort Sahl, the
famous night club entertainer (1960), Bob Dylan (1964), Federico Fellini
(1965), Buckminster Fuller (1966), Stanley Kubrick (1966), Albert Einstein
(1973), Gandhi (1976), King Hussein of Jordan (1983), Dizzy Gillespie (1990),
and Martin Scorsese (2000). And now, a boy from the Bronx—Michael Savage!

Famous Authors and Books Banned by Little People

I also receive encouragement from the prestige of belonging to another
group—the authors whose works have been banned by over-reaching governments
through the years.

- *Brave New World* by Aldous Huxley was banned in the country
  of Ireland in 1932.
- Voltaire's *Candide* was seized by US Customs in 1930 because
  they found it obscene.
- Another victim of banning in Ireland was *Gulliver's Travels* by
  Jonathan Swift.
- George Orwell's *1984* was banned by the USSR in 1950. Stalin
  thought it was an attack on his country by being a portrayal of its
  future. It was nearly banned by the USA and UK in the early sixties during the Cuban Missile Crisis. The ban in the Soviet Union
  was not lifted until 1990, and it was re-released after editing.

- Salman Rushdie's *The Satanic Verses* was banned in Bangladesh, India, and Singapore. It was also banned in Iran as blasphemy.
- *The Sorrows of Young Werther*, by Johann Wolfgang von Goethe, was banned in several European countries because of the encouragement of suicidal deaths that it showed the public.
- Jack London's *The Call of the Wild* was banned in both Yugoslavia and Italy.

Why do these works—and their banishment during various time periods in history—encourage me? As I said already, it is a privilege to be part of such a group. But there is another reason. In the West, at least, none of these books are banned anymore. The censors failed to achieve any lasting victory over the freedom of writers and speakers.

I fight to make sure that my history is the same as theirs.

This is my story, and the story of an attack on everyone's freedom of speech in the West. It is a story of great importance to every one of you, no matter what your politics. As the Russian newspaper *Pravda* has pointed out, under Obama, "the American descent into Marxism is happening with breathtaking speed" as we experience "the surrender of their freedoms and souls, to the whims of their elites and betters."[8] Our basic civil freedoms are at stake.

As this book goes to press I have filed a final demand for an apology, retraction and legal fees from the British government. This will be a long and costly battle but I will continue to fight for my right to speak freely (as well as yours!)—with "God's help and your support; may God bless America."

Preface Notes

1 Melanie Phillips, "Beware this Saudi deal to help bail out Britain. It comes with a devastating IOU," *Daily Mail*, November 10, 2008, http://www.dailymail.co.uk/news/article-1084335/Beware-Saudi-deal-help-bail-Britain-It-comes-devastating-IOU.html#ixzz0Oltnlotj (Last viewed on August 17, 2009).

2 Jemima Khan, "Britain's love affair with the Saudi kingdom,"*The Telegraph*, November 4, 2007, http://www.telegraph.co.uk/comment/3643778/Britains-love-affair-with-the-Saudi-kingdom.html (Last viewed on August 17, 2009).

3 Alasdair Palmer, "Why must we bow to the intolerant ways of Islam?" *The Telegraph*, August 15, 2009, http://www.telegraph.co.uk/news/newstopics/religion/6034998/Why-must-we-bow-to-the-intolerant-ways-of-Islam.html (Last viewed August 17, 2009).

4 Drew Zahn, "Hacker Attack Disables Michael Savage Website," *World Net Daily*, August 23, 2009, http://www.wnd.com/index.php?fa=PAGE.view &pageId=107683, (Last viewed on August 23, 2009).

5 James Chapman and Ian Drury, "Gaddafi embraces Lockerbie bomber and thanks his 'courageous friend' Gordon Brown for releasing him," *Mail Online,* August 22, 2009, http://www.dailymail.co.uk/news/article-1208001/Heros-welcome-Lockerbie-bomber-Megrahi-slaughtered-270.html (Last viewed on August 22, 2009).

6 Jason Allardyce, August 30, 2009, http://www.timesonline.co.uk/tol/news/politics/article6814939.ece, Last viewed on August 31, 2009.

7 Kelefa Sanneh, "Party of One: Michael Savage, Unexpurgated," *The New Yorker*, August 3, 2009, 53.

8 Stanislov Mishin, "American Capitalism Gone with a Wimper,"*Pravda*, April 27, 2009. http://english.pravda.ru/print/opinion/columnists/107459-american_capitalism-0 Last viewed on August 11, 2009.

Banned In Britain

1

Savage Strikes Back

I have led a rather elusive and reclusive life. But after being put on a list with murderers, racists, and terrorists–as a direct result of the British Government's unilateral verdict that she pronounced on me without ever giving me a day in court–I had to get 24-hour-security.

I mention this because many–friends, enemies, and neutrals–sometimes assume that I'm enjoying the publicity. People hear me on *The Savage Nation* getting heated in my own defense (which I think is more than understandable) and get the bizarre idea that I am happy to be talking about this crisis in my life. That is simply wrong. Just because I'm standing up for myself doesn't mean that I'm enjoying this right now. I take no joy in this attack and I do not revel at having to defend myself.

Don't confuse a man who is defending his honor with a man who wants to defend his honor. Don't assume a man who is standing up for himself is not a man who would rather be left alone.

When you push a man into the corner you have to expect a man who has character and self-respect to stand up for himself. Enjoyment has nothing to do with it.

I believe that I have a lot to stand up for, not only for principle but also on a personal level as well. I have spent my entire life establishing a fine reputation. I don't care whether a small band of haters is opposed to my viewpoints. There are tens of millions of Americans who love my viewpoints. They agree with them because they represent them. I am their voice and their advocate. They have bought hundreds of thousands of copies of my books in hardcover. I've had four *New York Times* bestsellers. My profile in *The New Yorker* puts me in league with luminaries such as Fellini, Einstein, Gandhi, and many other major artistic and literary figures–none of whom was a murderer or a terrorist!

Before that, I spent 20 years as an expert on nutrition, herbal medicine and alternative health. I earned two Masters' degrees from the University of Hawaii, one in ethnobotany, and another in anthropology. And I earned my Ph.D in nutritional ethnomedicine from the University of Berkley in 1978. I was also a pioneer in that field. Before that I saved many plants from annihilation in rain-forests. I was ahead of my time in that regard. I've done very good things for the earth and for the people of the earth.

All of this was a complete shock and surprise. Who knew that this guy from the Bronx would wind up being hated by an entire government? Who would think it? You get on the radio and you speak for fifteen years, and you say things that people both love and hate.

But whoever thought that the British government would come out and ban me from Britain? I never thought it would happen. I thought maybe I'd be banned from Syria. I thought maybe I'd be banned from Iran, maybe Venezuela. And I thought I'd probably be banned from North Korea. But I never imagined I'd be banned from the land of the Magna Carta. Never in a million years.

So this is a big deal to me. I will not be silent and passive so that some unknown bureaucrat in England can spread falsehoods about me, associate me with murderers and terrorists, and enact charges against me without a trial. I realize Britain is a sovereign nation and has the authority to prevent people from coming into their country. But the fact remains that civilized nations owe it to one another to respect and protect rather than libel and banish their citizens unless something has gone seriously wrong. Consider the full text that is written on a British passport:

> Her Britannic Majesty's Secretary of State Requests and requires in
> the Name of Her Majesty all those whom it may concern to allow
> the bearer to pass freely without let or hindrance, and to afford the
> bearer such assistance and protection as may be necessary.

Does this sound like a "privilege" that can be withheld on a whim? Not at all! Furthermore, it is quite obvious that one element of this decision was an attempt to do something "tough" in order to try to compensate for a host of problems and scandals besetting the Labour Party. We will see in the next chapter Jacqui Smith's own problems with illegal aliens working for the Home Office and her use of funds for pornography and other scandals. Speaker Michael Martin resigned from office at about the same time that the British government banned me–the first House speaker to step down in more than 300 years. The next election in Britain must be held before June 2010 and the Labour Party is likely to suffer greatly since the *Daily Telegraph* has published stories exposing high levels of corruption in claiming expenses.[1]

It's no wonder then that a local San Francisco columnist wrote about what happened to me: "As chickens know, when pecked, you peck another." It looks like this whole "name and shame" list was, at best, showmanship that was more motivated by a need for good PR rather than a genuine and reasoned attempt to make Britain safer. Furthermore, it also looks like a white male was included to appear racially and religiously "balanced"–that is, to placate radical Muslims.

So what was I to do?

Savage Calls on Hillary: My Letter to the Secretary of State

One of the first steps I took was one that wasn't pleasant to me. I had my lawyer write a letter appealing to "The Honorable Hillary Rodham-Clinton." This was mocked by some because I am opposed to many of Hillary Clinton's policies. And I've said so forcefully, and often.

But why should that matter? One of my big objections to Hillary Clinton, after all, is that she doesn't really believe in the First Amendment or free speech, so here is her chance to prove me wrong. Here is her chance to show that she believes the First Amendment respects all people. Here is her chance to practice equality before the law. She is, after all, the Secretary of State for all Americans–including me. And she actually volunteered for this position in the Obama Administration. So she has obligated herself to carry out those duties, whether or not they are on behalf of friends or foes.

This was her chance to shine.

But she hasn't.

Both the United States and the United Kingdom have signed and ratified the

International Covenant on Civil and Political Rights (ICCPR). So I appealed to its provisions in my letter to Clinton. My exercise of my rights acknowledged in the First Amendment to the Constitution ought not to be the basis of restricting my travel to England, especially when both countries are signatories to the ICCPR. The letter singles out especially Article 19, section 2,

> Everyone shall have the right to freedom of expression; this right shall include freedom to seek, receive and impart information and ideas of all kinds, regardless of frontiers, either orally, in writing or in print, in the form of art, or through any other media of his choice.

My request to Mrs. Clinton was simple and straightforward.

She was told by my lawyer, on my behalf, that I "…respectfully demand that you call upon the government of the United Kingdom to rescind the arbitrary and capricious decision to ban Mr. Savage, a U.S. citizen, from entering the United Kingdom." The letter also pointed out some important aspects of the incident, including,

> The United Kingdom is punishing Mr. Savage for what he says in the United States and not what he has said or intends to say in the United Kingdom. Mr. Savage's radio show is not broadcast in the United Kingdom. I doubt many British citizens ever heard of Mr. Savage until after the May 5 ban. It is extremely suspicious that the Home Secretary's office would select an American radio talk show host to place on their so-called "least wanted list," when that individual has never taken steps to enter their country.

We pointed out that I have been on the radio fifteen years and have never once called for violence, nor has my radio show ever instigated violence. The letter also pointed out that other obligations made the legal grounds for the Home Office's decision questionable. England has signed the European Convention on Human Rights. Article Ten of that document states:

> Everyone has the right to freedom of expression. This right shall include freedom to hold opinions and to receive and impart infor-

mation and ideas without interference by public authority and regardless of frontiers.

Not only that, but the Convention established the European Court of Human Rights. It had ruled in a court case that "freedom of expression constitutes one of the essential foundations of a democratic society," and that this freedom was not only for that which is popularly acceptable, but also for expressions "that *offend, shock,* or *disturb*" (emphasis added).

My letter ended by reiterating my initial request and then making one more. The letter written on my behalf again "respectfully" demanded that

> ...you and the U.S. Department of State take all necessary steps to call on the government of the United Kingdom, and more particularly, the office of the Home Secretary Jacqui Smith, to rescind the aforementioned ban.

But it also added a request for the State Department to "...determine how and what specific criteria the Home Office applied to place Mr. Savage on the aforementioned list. Please keep the undersigned informed of the steps you plan to take and are taking."

I didn't stop with the letter. I talked about it on my show to get my listeners to write and call their representatives to ask Mrs. Clinton to do the right thing. That day, on my program, I said,

> There comes a time in every man's life when you have to get down to brass tacks. This is it. My name has been put on a list with murderers. I want my name off the list. Now, who do I turn to? Well, first I must tell you that I turn to my own government. It doesn't matter that they don't like my politics. The fact that they abhor my politics is why they should help me. Voltaire said, "I do not agree with what you have to say but I'll defend to the death your right to say it." Voltaire was taught by all philosophy professors to all college students for over a century. And, it used to be a credo of the liberals—that they will defend my right to say it. I am appealing to Hillary Clinton to act in this fashion because I'm an American citizen.

So far I have heard nothing. I can't say I am too surprised, though I had genuinely hoped Mrs. Clinton would rise to the occasion. Perhaps she still will. It would be great if she would surprise me.

The Legal Letters and The Secret Emails

I had no intention of stopping with this appeal to Hillary Clinton. It was an appropriate action to take and it ought to be effective, but I knew it probably would not work. I needed to use the law as best I could to clear my name and end this madness. I hired a major law firm, Olswang, one of the best in Great Britain. I found out that I did, indeed, have standing to sue Jacqui Smith in the British Courts. Before the month of May (2009) was over, I made UK newspaper headlines by arranging to sue her for 100,000 pounds and demanding an apology for her placing me on that list.

The initial letter from Olswang was sent to her on May 15 and offered to be willing to negotiate settlements out of court. It not only dealt with my placement on the list, but also with the press release that boldly referred to me as a "controversial daily radio host, who provoked others to commit crimes." It said:

> The allegations in the Press Release constitute serious and damaging defamatory allegations which are actionable under English law. The allegations are entirely false. At no time has our client provoked or sought to provoke others to commit crimes or serious criminal acts. If he were to issue proceedings in defamation, he would be likely to recover very substantial damages. In any such action, he would rely upon the highly aggravating circumstances of the publication of the Press Release, including:
>
> a. That publication was made by the Home Office and the Home Secretary respectively; coming from such respectable sources, the allegations would have been likely to have been readily believed by anyone who read the Press Release;
>
> b. The joining our client in the Press Release to:
>   i. an individual said to justify or glorify terrorist violence;

ii. an individual said to be responsible for a racist website
and promoting serious criminal activity and fostering
hatred;

iii. an individual said to have spent three decades in prison
for killing four soldiers and a four-year-old girl; and

iv. an individual said to be the leader of a violent gang that
beat migrants and posted films of their attacks on the
internet.

c. The wording of the Press Release which state it was expressly intended to "Name and shame" *inter alios* our client;

d. The fact that wide republication of the allegations was
inevitable and indeed was the intended outcome of the Press
Release; and

e. The fact that our client was not given any advance warning
of the Press Release or approached for comment in respect
of the allegations.

In such circumstances, our client has suffered very severe damage to
his reputation both in the United Kingdom and abroad.

I thought all this was quite compelling. I was not the only one. Even the prestigious *New Yorker* magazine said that the "immoderate quotations" possibly
assembled by mediamatters.org, that had somehow been sent to the Home Office
in Britain, were "misleading."[2] But the Home Office dug in their heels. They
wrote a completely unbelievable justification of their actions and my lawyers
replied point by point closing the loopholes they tried to slip through. The most
egregious issue was that their press release continued to libel me, claiming not
only that I sought "to provoke others to serious criminal acts and fostering
hatred," but that I had already "provoked others to commit crimes." They refused
to remove that statement from their website. My lawyers wrote,

It is particularly disappointing that you have responded on behalf
of your client in such unsatisfactory terms and… that your client

continues to publish the Press Release bearing in mind that your
client is a public authority under the Human Rights Act 1998 and
must act compatibly with inter alia Article 8 of the European
Convention on Human Rights. This includes a right to reputation.
In light of this, we consider it particularly important your client
respects our client's right to his reputation.

In addition to pursuing action in the courts, I also appealed directly to Prime
Minister Gordon Brown. Since I wrote to him before I actually knew that he was
directly involved in the decision to ban me, I had some small hope when I sent
him my letter:

The Prime Minister
10 Downing Street
London
SW1A2AA

8 June 2009

Dear Prime Minister:

*I am a radio show host in the United States. It is with great hope
that I write to you personally in relation to my treatment at the hands
of the former Home Secretary of the Government of the United
Kingdom, Ms Jacqui Smith.*

*As you may be aware, my name was recently included on a list of
individuals excluded from the United Kingdom. I understand the
policy under which the list was compiled is aimed at excluding individuals who stir-up, justify or glorify terrorism, encourage others to
participate in terrorist acts, engage in serious criminal activity or
encourage others in such activity or foster hatred which might lead to
inter-community violence in the United Kingdom.*

The decision to exclude me was plainly arbitrary and based on sound bites taken out of context. Moreover, the circumstances of the decision were on any view quite extraordinary.

I had made no request or given any indication that I proposed to visit the United Kingdom. Nonetheless, in or around December 2007, Ms Smith decided that I should be excluded from the United Kingdom.

No explanation has been offered as to why, of all the people in the world, I was selected for inclusion in the list of those so excluded. I was not consulted about or even informed of this decision at the time. The first I heard of this was when a press release was published on 5 May 2009.

The press release stated that I provoked others to commit crimes, that I sought to provoke others to serious criminal acts and that I fostered hatred which might lead to inter-community violence. These allegations are entirely untrue and extremely damaging. They are the subject of a defamation complaint against the Home Office and Ms Smith.

I am advised that these allegations are serious and that should I press my claim, I am likely to recover a very substantial award in damages. It is particularly disturbing that the press release containing these serious allegations has not been removed from the website of the Home Office despite repeated requests for this to be done and the complete failure of the Home Office to substantiate the allegations.

As you will understand, I was shocked to find my name listed with known murderers and terrorists. Shocked because in my 15-year radio career I have never advocated violence, nor have my words ever led to violence. Shocked because I was put on a list with a Hamas murderer who killed two young Israeli parents and then assaulted and killed their four-year old daughter with a rifle butt.

Shocked because my name was listed alongside Russian skinheads who glorified their murder of immigrants. It was particularly astonishing to me to see this happening in the land that I have so long admired, the land of the Magna Carta, the land of the mother of Parliaments and the land of the great Winston Churchill.

I am not an extremist. I am one of the most successful radio presenters in the United States with over 8 million listeners. Prior to becoming a radio presenter 15 years ago, I was a nutritionist and botanist. I have two Masters degrees in Medical Botany and Medical Anthropology and a Ph.D. in Epidemiology and Nutritional Ethno-Medicine from the University of California. I am the published author of over 20 books on these and related subjects.

As a scientist, I have helped to rescue rainforests in the South Pacific and I have catalogued hundreds of disappearing medicinal plants around the world (Kew Gardens is home to one of my rare collections of such plants). I am a passionate believer in free speech and it was a great honour to receive the prestigious Freedom of Speech Award by Talkers Magazine *in 2007.*

It has been said by Ms Smith that I advocated killing Muslims. She arrived at this conclusion by taking a statement I made completely out of context. I do not advocate killing Muslims or indeed anyone. I would never have been allowed to broadcast in the United States, nor would I have gained the popularity I have if I did or if my views otherwise provoked criminal acts or inter-community violence.

It seems to me that the most likely explanation for inclusion on the list was a desire that it be comprised of individuals of a mixture of ethnic origins, religions and nationalities and that I was identified and chosen solely to give the list a politically correct balance. That of course would be a wholly unfair and arbitrary way to proceed, particularly given that there were no proper grounds to exclude me.

I have been heartened by the vast support that I have received from the British public. It is clear that the British public value the fact that they live in a country that recognises free speech and are appalled at the arbitrary way in which a decision to exclude me has been made.

My listeners in the United States have also been shocked at the decision of Ms Smith. This has caused great damage to the reputation of the United Kingdom in my country. They, like me, cannot believe that the land of Magna Carta would have been reduced to this level.

One listener in particular wrote to me and told me that that he has cancelled a $5 million order for equipment manufactured in the United Kingdom and is also going to cancel two additional machinery orders valued at $2.2 million each in light of this decision.

I note that Ms Smith has resigned as Home Secretary and a new Home Secretary has taken over the role. I have today made an application to the new Home Secretary to reconsider my exclusion as a matter of urgency.

As a student of the history of the United Kingdom, I am aware that in 1945, Winston Churchill said the following:

> *"No socialist government conducting the entire life and industry of the country could afford to allow free, sharp, or violently worded expressions of public discontent. They would have to fall back on some form of Gestapo, no doubt very humanely directed in the first instance. And this would nip opinion in the bud; it would stop criticism as it reared its head, and it would gather all the power to the supreme party and the party leaders, rising like stately pinnacles above their vast bureaucracies of Civil servants, no longer servants and no longer civil."*

It seems to me that the illiberal attitude of Ms Smith in this case evokes the worst fears of Mr Churchill. I also noted that in your moving speech at the D-Day memorial on Saturday, you stated: "...tyranny may suppress, it cannot endure forever.., dictatorship may for a time have the power to dictate, but ... it will not in the end decide the course of the human journey."

I believe that little could be more tyrannical than the arbitrary and unfair exercise of power to exclude someone from a country for the purposes of suppressing free speech.

My family and I are both suffering from this grave injustice. For these reasons, I respectfully appeal to you to prevail upon the new Home Secretary to address the injustice caused by Ms Smith and remove forthwith my name from the list of excluded individuals.

Yours faithfully,

Michael Savage

I never heard anything from the Prime Minister–which was not a complete surprise. We did finally get a reply from the Home Office on August 5. They acted as self-righteous as ever. They repeated the unspeakable lie that I have called for "the murder of Muslims, and claimed that I was guilty until proven innocent, saying, "The onus is on your client to publicly renounce the statements which formed the basis of the decision to exclude him." If I wanted to be unbanned, then "Any such repudiation must be genuine and comprehensive, and persuade my client that this is a true shift of position."

They were not backing down from their license to libel. They were adding to the insult to injury, not only banning me, but preaching at me to recant, as if I was a heretic brought before a medieval inquisitor. I had to recite the multi-cultural creed to be let back in.

My lawyers replied we had already demonstrated that "our client does not believe that it is right to kill any Muslims, it is simply outrageous that you suggest that either we or our client should *justify calling for the murder of Muslims.'* As we have made clear, that is not something our client would ever seek to do."

Moreover, we ask that you explain how our client can repudiate views which are not his own and why he should satisfy your client that there has been *"a true shift of position"* when the only issue has been the misunderstanding by your client as to what his views are. To ask him to do so is plainly oppressive. We have explained to you what his true views are to you and given you every assurance about his conduct were he to come to the United Kingdom. That must be sufficient for your client. We do not understand how any reasonable Home Secretary could require anything further. We ask that you set out how you can justify such a stance.

By the time they wrote this letter, my lawyers had uncovered new evidence. They had used Freedom of Information laws in Britain to force the government to reveal emails and other documents that had never been intended to be read by the public. These communications revealed that I was, as I had guessed, chosen for the list because I am white and non-Muslim. They also revealed how far the British government was involved in the decision to ban me for "balance." Not only the Home Office, but the Foreign Secretary and the Prime Minister himself, wanted me on the list. Why? One email, sent on November 27, 2008 from a Home Office official, said clearly why: *"I can understand that disclosure of the decision would help provide a balance of types of exclusion cases."* Another document said, *"We will want to ensure that the names disclosed reflect the broad range of cases and are not all Islamic extremists. Otherwise the exercise could play into the hands of radicals who allege falsely that the unacceptable behaviours policy is targeted specifically at the Muslim community."*

One bureaucrat in the Home Office even said of their plan to libel me, *"I think we could be accused of duplicity in naming him."* Yet not only was the Home Office behind the duplicity, but as another document stated, *"Both the FS [Foreign Secretary] and PM [Prime Minister] are firmly behind listing and naming such people."*[3]

These secret emails were amazing. I gained partial vindication. I had been right all along–that I was chosen simply because I was white and non-Muslim. But the Home Office, as their letter revealed, even when caught in such abuse of power, was still refusing to reverse their decision or admit to any wrongdoing.

So my lawyers pointed out several things:

> You will note from the letter that we are still awaiting a response to Part 3 of our client's Freedom of Information request, which we understand has been delayed due to the need to liaise with a number of individuals and the amount of material that needs to be collated. Despite the fact that we are still awaiting a full response from the UK Border Agency, we thought it appropriate to draw your attention to a number of matters arising from the information that we have received so far, as follows.

The first point my lawyers made was that the documentation of their researcher stated categorically, *"There is no evidence of [our client] advocating or inciting violence."* Yet,

> Despite the conclusion by the primary researcher that *"there is no evidence of [our client] advocating or inciting violence,"* the final version of the Home Office's submission to the Home Secretary dated December 2008 (attached) concluded that the Home Secretary should exclude our client *"on the ground that his presence here would not be conducive to the public good because he has engaged in unacceptable behavior by seeking to provoke others to serious criminal acts and foster hatred which might lead to intercommunity violence."* It is not clear from the papers provided by the UK Border Agency how this conclusion was reached.

> There is certainly no basis for such a conclusion in the papers provided by the UK Border Agency. Indeed, as the primary researcher concluded, there is no evidence of our client "advocating or inciting violence," nor of our client *"seeking to provoke others to serious criminal acts and fostering hatred which might lead to inter-community violence."*

So not only were the Home Office's statements about me wrong, but *according to their own research* they were making unfounded claims.

The second issue my lawyers raised is that these bureaucrats claimed they couldn't find my address to inform me! My lawyers pointed out that *"this demonstrates the lack of care with which the Home Office and the former Home Secretary made their decision to exclude our client."* How could the entire British government be incapable of finding the address of a popular radio host in the United States? You can find almost anyone with just a basic Google search!

Other points had to do with the fact that I was selected for the list by a kind of racial profiling:

3. It is clear from an email between Home Office officials timed at 12.48 on 27 November 2008 (page 38) that there had been discussion within the Home Office that disclosure of the decision to exclude our client *"would help provide balance of types of exclusion cases."* This is wholly improper. The Home Secretary had no business whatsoever having regard to *"balance"* when either determining any decision as to exclusion or drawing up the list. We ask that you explain this reference and how your client considered it to be justified.

4. We note from an email between Home Office officials timed at 2.20 pm on 1 December 2008 (page 40) that the author of that email was of the opinion that the Home Office *"could be accused of duplicity"* by naming our client and not other individuals on the exclusion list. Despite these concerns, the Home Office decided to name our client in the published list. Please explain the basis on which this decision was reached.

5. It is apparent from the version of the Home Office submissions dated December 2008 (page 42) that the decision to make our client's exclusion public was made on the basis that it would *"help to reassure the public that the exclusion process was working effectively"* and because the Home Office wanted to ensure that the names disclosed *"reflected a broad range of UB cases and are not all Islamist extremists."* Please therefore confirm that our client was included on the published list to provide the list with balance.

My lawyers then pointed to *The New Yorker* profile which dealt with the quotations the Home Office was using. They pointed out that the writer, Kelefa Sanneh, was not ideologically aligned with me at all.

> Mr. Sanneh is plainly independent and politically no natural supporter of the views of our client. Nonetheless, he has taken the trouble to carry out detailed research about him and formed a balanced view. This is wholly different to the approach of the Home Office in selecting a few random extracts of what our client has stated out of context, from which it has formed a deeply misleading impression of our client. As stated by Mr. Sanneh in his article:

>> *"The immoderate quotes meticulously catalogued by the liberal media-watchdog site mediamatters.org are accurate but misleading, insofar as they reduce a willfully erratic broadcast to a series of political brick bats."*

Our letter concluded with a respectful request for the Home Secretary to "review this material carefully and give it very significant weight." We asked that he "reconsider his decision," but also said that, "In the meantime, all our client's rights are reserved."

British law about defamation is rather different than our laws in America. My lawyers wrote me a lengthy explanation. Here is part of it:

> Dear Michael

> Further to my email to you of Friday, I set out our views on the merits of your defamation action against the Home Office and the Home Secretary, Ms Jacqui Smith, personally. I am sorry that this is rather long. As you will understand the law in this area is somewhat complex and I believe that it is necessary and will be helpful that you are fully apprised of this and the potential risks. At the end of this email I provide a summary of our advice which I hope is convenient for you. Suffice to say at this stage, I believe that you have a strong case although as with virtually all litigation, there *are* some risks.

I will provide separately our views on your case against the Home Secretary in respect of challenging the banning order itself.

The nature of defamation law in England

Before I address the detail of your claim, I thought it would be helpful to say something regarding the nature of defamation law and defamation actions in England.

As you will no doubt be aware, defamation law in England is somewhat notorious. There have been a number of high profile defamation actions over the last 20 or so years. It has often been said that the law of defamation in England is very favourable *to* claimants (or plaintiffs as you would say in the United States). Indeed, this has led to courts in your country refusing to enforce defamation awards made here and further calls in various states for statutory provisions to be enacted to grant further protection to prevent enforcement.

It is true that our defamation law lacks a number of features of the law in the United States which make it hard to succeed in a case. Most particularly, we do not have the First Amendment of the Constitution (although we do have Article 10 of the European Convention on Human Rights which grants a form of freedom of expression) and we have only a highly diluted equivalent of the decision of the Supreme Court of the United States in *Sullivan* establishing a public figure defence.

Bearing these matters in mind, I now turn to the specific issues in the action.

The Defendants

The letter from the Treasury Solicitor states that the Home Office would be the appropriate defendant in this action. It is not entirely clear what they are saying here. However, if they are contending that no action is possible against Ms Smith personally, we do not agree. In defamation law, responsibility for publication can extend to any person who was responsible for the publication complained of. In this case, since Ms Smith plainly authorised the publication of the Press Release, we believe that she should be personally liable for it.

The Defences

In their letter, the Treasury Solicitor advances on behalf of the Home Office two defences to the defamation claim. Firstly, there is a proposed defence of justification. Secondly, there is a defence of qualified privilege. I will consider each in turn.

Justification

In defamation, the defence of justification is a claim that the words complained of are materially true. In assessing this defence, there are three steps:

(a) What are the allegations complained of?
(b) What is the true meaning of those allegations?
(c) Can it be shown that those allegations–in their true meaning–are materially true?

The Allegations Complained of

We consider that in the Press Release, there are in reality three separate allegations against you.

(a) that you provoked others to commit crimes (that is, we would say, that you actually caused other to commit crimes)
(b) that you sought to provoke others to serious criminal acts (that is, we would say, that you intended to provoke others to commit serious criminal acts, regardless of whether they committed them); and
(c) you fostered hatred which might lead to inter-community violence.

The Treasury Solicitor sets out what we consider to be a rather confused case regarding whether the words complained of are materially true. In particular, they cite six extracts ("the Extracts") of words which you are alleged to have stated. I am sure that these Extracts have been taken entirely out of context and that in each case, if the full context were understood, the effect of the words may be somewhat different. We will in due course have to establish the full context of each of these Extracts with you in detail. However, even if this is not the case and we take these words as they are set out (and the rest of this advice will proceed on that basis), I believe that you have a good case for the following reasons:

The Extracts do not seem to amount to any provocation to commit criminal offences whatsoever. The Treasury Solicitor refers to the Public Order Act 1986. It is true that this is a fairly draconian piece of legislation. It is also true that if you said any of these Extracts in the United Kingdom (subject to their true context) this may have constituted offences in this country. But you did not say any of the Extracts in the United Kingdom, you stated then in the United States where, I understand it was perfectly legal for you to do so. Accordingly, I find it very hard to understand how any of these Extracts could be said to justify the allegations. For this reason, I believe that there is a good prospect that a judge would find in our favour and not allow the issue of whether these Extracts justify the allegations go to the jury.

Defence of Qualified Privilege

The Treasury Solicitor also advances a defence of qualified privilege. This is a somewhat technical defence to a defamation action which can apply where the words complained of are untrue. The law provides that on certain occasions (for example making a report to the police), defamatory communications are permissible provided they are not made with actual malice. The Treasury Solicitor contends that the Press Release was made on such an occasion.

The basis for this contention is not very clearly set out in the letter. However, they seem (as stated at paragraph 8 of the letter) to believe an occasion of qualified privilege arises in this case for two reasons.

> (a) Because Ms Smith "announced by a written statement in the House of Commons on 28 October 2008 ... that Government would inform the public of individuals who are excluded from the United Kingdom."

> (b) Because section 15 and schedule 1, paragraph 7 of the Defamation Act 1996 ("the Act") provides for such a defence.

I will deal with each in turn.

We do not believe it likely that the announcement by Ms Smith in the House of Commons referred to provides any basis for a defence of qualified privilege. Firstly, although the law is somewhat uncertain in this regard, we do not believe it likely that the courts would hold that a member of the Government can establish her own occasion of qualified privilege simply by making a statement in the House of Commons.

Secondly, in fact, in her statement on 28 October 2008 she did not announce that she would name those excluded, far less the reasons for the exclusion. She merely said that she would "[c]onsider in all future cases whether it would be in the public interest to disclose that an individual has been excluded with a presumption to inform the public" (indeed six of those excluded were not named). Accordingly, we do not see how the statement provides the basis for any defence of qualified privilege in naming you and providing the (factually erroneous) reasons for your exclusion.

In terms of the defence relied on under the Act, this applies to any "fair and accurate copy of or extract from matter published by or on the authority of a government or legislature anywhere in the world". However, we would be extremely surprised if this applied here. It is clear that this defence is intended to apply only to any further republication of any report from the Government (for example in a newspaper). It does not apply to the original report from the Government itself. If it did, this would essentially confer on Government a broad immunity from defamation actions which has never been suggested or contemplated.

For these reasons, we believe that the defences of qualified privilege contended would be very likely to fail and we believe that there would be good prospects that they would be struck out by a judge.

I did not restrict my efforts, however, to the British political and legal system. Even before my British attorneys sent the first letter to the Home Office, I also began another strategy. My faith in the courts and in civil governments has been shaken too much for me to rest my fate in their hands alone. I began interviewing in the British media, as well as the American media.

The British Press was already skeptical about Jacqui Smith due to a number of ways in which she had shown herself to be incompetent. I decided I needed to take the battle to her own backyard, not only legally, but also in the public record.

The day after I was "named and shamed" by the British government, I gave a phone interview on a TV news show on Sky News, and also a televised interview with the BBC. In both interviews, I reiterated my point that I am not a murderer or a terrorist, nor am I one who advocates murder or terrorism. The Home Office's list is libelous; it declares things about me that are simply not true.

Later, I was able to get an interview on BBC radio with Victoria Derbyshire, someone with an extremely popular show in Britain. That interview went very well, though at first it was obvious to me, from Derbyshire's tone, that she had very little respect for the "shock-jock" she thought she was interviewing. But I persevered and, it seemed to me and my wife that her tone changed as she realized that I was a real person with real accomplishments, such as my graduate degrees in hard sciences.[4]

The British Government Versus the Truth: Responding to the Charges

In these interviews with British news, CNN, and elsewhere, I worked to undo the damage that the British Government was causing me as best I could.

Jacqui Smith's accusations are, to some extent, self-condemning. She accused me of "seeking to provoke others to serious criminal acts and fostering hatred which might lead to inter-community violence." The claim that I was seeking to provoke anyone to commit a criminal act, let alone a serious criminal act, was simply false. It made a claim about my motives that was not only false, but plainly beyond the ability of the British Government to determine.

The other part, however–the part about "fostering hatred" and the "inter-community violence" to which it might lead–was actually a more accurate description of herself than of me. I brought this up at the end of my interview with Victoria Derbyshire.

I asked of Jacqui Smith, "Why is she taking those words and blaring them out there? Isn't she promoting violence? Isn't she the one disseminating violence?" The words I was referring to were my statements ripped out of any kind of context and published in a way that artificially isolated them so that she could then claim that these fragments represented my entire show.

As I said in the interview,

> None of my words have ever led to violence. Ever. Some of them are offensive–I admit that. Some of them are violently worded. Some of them are sharp. But that is not violence, per se. Moreover, the most important thing is that all of these statements were taken out of context. I don't want to be judged by twenty-second sound bites taken out of context.

By publishing and drawing attention to statements in isolation, the British government was doing more than I ever had to promote hatred. Such sound bites, as such, were never actually part of the radio show. They were part of a context where a great deal more was said.

The evidence that proves I don't say hateful things about Islam is that I have regular Islamic listeners who don't hate me or find me hateful of them at all. Professional Islam-promoting groups like CAIR may have an axe to grind, but individual Muslims without an agenda are as prone to become fans of the show as anyone else.

I summarized the truth to Derbyshire: *"I have supported the five major religions for the last fifteen years on the radio. I was talking about the great religions, including Islam, beginning in 1994. I'm a great supporter of organized religion."* The problem with an interview, however, is that I do not have the ability to immediately prove what I say.

But in this book I do. Allow me to recount what I have said on the air about Islam and how I have interacted with Muslim callers.

Some Muslims Who Have Been on The Savage Nation

To start with, on November 21, 2006, I mentioned on the air that I have an acquaintance from Morocco *"...who is more terrified of the radical Muslims than I am"* because he had lost relatives to them. In fact, I have reported that there have been thousands of deaths of non-radical Muslims in Algeria because of violence by radical Al-Qaeda-types who attempt to forcefully convert.

In Palestine, too, the violence is not coming from all Muslims. I commented on July 14, 2006, *"I've been to Israel, not recently, but, believe me, the Western educated Palestinians would just as soon run a business and make a living. They don't need warfare. Most of this is coming from the fanatics."*

In November 29, 2006 I spoke with a Muslim who had just heard a Rabbi on my show who defended evolution as compatible with religion. Here is how I introduced the interview:

> There are areas of unity between the religions and I think we need to strengthen those. We need to strengthen those areas of unity. Maybe this AM radio show can help do that. Mohammed from Orlando, welcome back to the program. Now, you heard the rabbi from New York and his views of evolution and creation. Do you agree with them?

He did. What followed was a great conversation, disagreeing with Christian creationists who denied evolution was possible. We discussed how Judaism and Islam could be interpreted in ways that allowed for scientific findings. We ended the conversation laughing: *"Mohammed, bless you. Alechem Salam. Thanks for listening to* The Savage Nation.*"*

A year earlier, I had a Muslim call me and talk about how Hollywood's immorality was challenging to a faithful Muslim trying to raise a family. He claimed that fellow Muslims, as well as Christians and Jews, were giving him morally-compromised advice, claiming one should take time to *have fun* before getting married.

> I'm thirty years old, I'm married, and I have a daughter. But you talk to guys my age in the city of Houston and when I tell them that I'm married, whether those guys are Christians or Jews or Muslims, they all look at me like I'm, like I'm crazy, you know. They tell me, "Oh, you're way too young to get married; you're way too young to raise a family."

The caller, who was also named Mohammed, also told me of Islamic friends in Europe who felt pressured by the immorality there. I ended the call with this piece of advice:

> Yeah, well you stick to your faith, Mohammed; you're on the right track. It's God's way, that's my opinion. Let me send you copy of *Liberalism is a Mental Disorder* for your reading pleasure. So there it is. It's an interesting story: "Muslim says Savage is right on the cultural war that is going on."

This sort of conversation is not rare. On March 27, 2007, I got a call from another Muslim caller named Mehmet who had emigrated from Turkey in 1993 and who had been listening to the show for three years. He described himself as believing in "eighty percent" of what I said, and someone who affirmed American values. "My question to you," he said, "is: can I be a Muslim and still support American values in this country?" I replied:

> Sure you can, absolutely. That's what I said all along. Look, it's like saying "Can I be a Jew and still support American values?" "Can I be a Buddhist and still support American values?" "Can I be a Hindu?" "Can I be an atheist?" Yes!

That's what America is all about. It is freedom of religion and freedom to be non-religious. That's what makes the country great, its
freedom.

As we talked, I realized Mehmet was concerned about some things he had
heard me say about the founding of the United States and the importance of
Christianity. He thought that those statements might mean that a Muslim could
not be a true American. No, that was not what I was saying at all!

"*When I say that the founding documents of America are based upon Christian
doctrine,*" I explained, "*I am talking about the fundamental humanity of Christianity,
which transcends that single religion.*" That fundamental humanity "*is incorporat-
ed in virtually every religion, including Islam, including Judaism, including
Buddhism, because if you read the Buddhist tractate which I have done intimately, it's
all about the same things.*"

They all come down to the Golden Rule, which I believe is the essence of
every religion.

If you boiled most religions down, Mehmet, when they are not
fanatically interpreted, every religion can be reduced to one statement: "Do not do unto others as you would have them not do unto
you." Or, "Do unto others as you would have them do unto you."
Let's put it that way. Isn't that fundamentally what every religion
teaches?

We talked a little longer and I kept emphasizing that everybody knows "the
basic rules of living with people" no matter what their religion is. "Even an athe-
ist knows it's not right to take a penny out of another man's pocket that's not
yours. That basic knowledge is available to Muslims, as well as Christians or athe-
ists." All can live by American values.

Another caller phoned *The Savage Nation* to agree with me about the threat
of Islamic extremism. Douglas, who had been a Muslim for eighteen years, called
on November 5, 2006 from Cincinnati, Ohio, and told me that, "*there are a lot
of misrepresentations inside the Islam faith with some of the whack-jobs across the
planet.*" He was confident that these terrorism supporters were misrepresenting
the Koran.

I told Doug that non-Muslims, like myself, didn't understand how extremists were able to *"rip off a religion like this and defame it, frankly, in the name of Allah."* I didn't understand how they could get away with doing that.

Douglas agreed: *"It's unbelievable, but, but, what they've got to understand is that a lot of us speak out against this, but I think too often people look for these so-called leaders, and they just need to look at the everyday Muslim who speaks out against this nonsense."*

I really liked that answer. Here is how I ended our conversation:

> Beautiful. You know what? You give me courage. You give me the courage for the future of America because I can't believe that the average man–Muslim, Christian, Jewish, Buddhist, Hindu, or agnostic–would want to burn a country to the ground. I just can't believe that they want to take a nation like this and destroy it. Thank you my friend, I'm glad you're a listener, frankly.

Also, soon after the horrible tragedy of September 11, 2001, I saw a Muslim leader on TV speaking for peace and tolerance, and condemning violence. I was so impressed with him that I arranged to have him on *The Savage Nation*. Here is part of that interview:

Savage: Let's go immediately to an honored guest, a Sheikh Kabbani. I welcome you to *The Savage Nation*, welcome, welcome, welcome.

Sheikh: Thank you very much. Thank you.

Savage: Sheikh, I saw you speak today on Fox News channel and I was so impressed with your words and I don't want to put words in your mouth, nor do I want to lead you in any way, but I just want to introduce you. You head up the Islamic Supreme Council of America is that correct?

Sheikh: That's correct.

Savage: And what does that organization, what does that body basically do?

Sheikh: That is an educational organization that speaks about anything about Islamic authority and knowledge and expressions, and building bridges

with the administration and with different offices–introducing them to the real message of Islam, the traditional Islam and the mainstream Islam.

Savage: What impressed me was when you were on Fox, Sheikh, was that you said that there are one billion people on planet Earth who ascribe to Islam, but you said that a small number–I think you said 500,000–have sort of misinterpreted what Islam is. Isn't that more or less what you said?

Sheikh: Nearly, that is what I said. That there are the majority of Muslims around the world–the one billion and something–who are peaceful Muslims and following the traditional Islam. But there is a very small minority that are inventing, for their own purposes and their own interests and benefit, a new sect of Islam at the beginning of this century. And it's becoming more developed today. It's becoming more radical and more violent, suiting the purposes of these terrorists to use it–cutting and pasting from the holy Koran or cutting and pasting the holy of prophets of Allah.

Savage: Cutting and pasting. I like what you mean by that! Of course other religions have done the same and will continue to do so. I saw an article, Sheikh, in the *Telegraph* of London, which I read earlier on *The Savage Nation*, from a person who was a torturer who worked with the Taliban. But he said something interesting, and I would like to read one sentence. He was talking about the rules called the Taliban and Mullah Omar in particular, and he said it's the first time in Afghanistan's history that the lower classes are governing and by force. He said that there are no educated people in this administration, totally backward and illiterate. He said, although they call themselves Mullahs, they have no idea of Islam. Is that a factual statement?

Sheikh: He might; he might. You know, today, with all this Internet access and with all this different movement around the world, that they've claiming themselves that they are speaking on behalf of Muslims, now becoming every student or every uneducated person, he read a little bit of Koran or read a little bit of Islamic knowledge and he consider himself becoming an authority and he becoming to give verdict and wants to people to follow him and establish for himself a group of people following him.

Savage: He says, nowhere does it say men must have beards or women cannot be educated. In fact, Koran says people must seek education, is that correct?

Sheikh: The first verse that was revealed to the Prophet in the Holy Koran means *educate yourself and read.* The first word in the Holy Koran means read all Prophet. Read. Learn your people how to read. Learn them how to write. And that's why Prophet Mohammed, at the beginning of the time, he asked his companion that, "Who knows how to read and write, let him teach the others how to read and write because knowledge is very important." And he said, "Seek knowledge even if it is in China," meaning, even if its afar, wherever the knowledge can exist, go after knowledge and education.

Savage: But certainly, a modern American Muslim, or a modern Muslim in any part of the world, would not prohibit women from an education. I think we would agree on that.

Sheikh: It's not only modern Muslim in any part of the world or in America. Islam, in general, does not prohibit, but it encourages women to study. And the wife of Prophet was the one of the best scholar in her time, and she was teaching all the men in the time of Prophet.

Savage: Well, frankly, I am relieved, to be honest with you. I can't say I am knowledgeable about Islam. I am not. But the fact of the matter is we're facing individuals who've declared war on America, who have put the statement that "we are doing it for Allah." You certainly wouldn't agree with that would you?

Sheikh: That's the problem: it's very easy to say "I am doing it for Allah," but he is doing it for the devil–for Satan not for Allah.

Savage: Sheikh–boy do we need to hear your voice more than ever before!

After some more questions and comments, I signed off with Sheikh Kabbani saying, *"If we ever needed the words of peace, we need them today, Sheik, and I thank you so much for being a guest on* The Savage Nation. *And I just want to say,* Alechem Salam, *to you."*

The Voice of Inter-Community Violence or Peace?

So there you have it. Are these quotations likely to cause inter-community violence? Do they sound like the voice of someone who wants to encourage serious criminal acts? What gave Jacqui Smith the right to publish her sound-bites and make them the final word on my character? In a court of law, the accused gets to both explain the prosecution's evidence against him, so that the court sees that it does not lead to the conclusion the prosecution is arguing for, and to present his own evidence in his own defense that the prosecution has overlooked.

It shouldn't be that surprising that *The New Yorker* magazine was able to see who I really am. No wonder *The New Yorker* wrote in the profile of me that *"the immoderate quotes"* a liberal website had *"meticulously catalogued"* were *"accurate but misleading."*

Not only do my interviews, quoted above, show that I have great respect for Islam, as I do for all religions, but they show that I have Muslim listeners who know this is true. When I spoke to the BBC interviewer and told her I have supported Islam and all major religions, this was not some recent pose I adopted to look better to the world. It was the consistent message of *The Savage Nation* from the beginning. Jacqui Smith has taken sharply-worded reactions to violent Islamic extremism, and a suicidal multi-cultural ethic that drives policy-makers around the globe to refuse to acknowledge or deal with that threat. She took these words (or someone did so for her) and deliberately isolated them to make it look like I believe and advocate things that are the very opposite of what *The Savage Nation* stands for.

Read those last two sentences carefully. They show how wrong her actions are. She may claim to be dealing with hate and encouragement to criminal activity, but she is, in fact, trying to suppress a voice that strongly disagrees with her policies regarding immigration and national security. This is not about protecting Britain from violence, but about protecting the Labour Party—as well as their soul-mates in America, whether Republican or Democrat—from political criticism. She (or someone) wants to *marginalize dissent*, and I am an experiment in a new method of doing so.

The BBC interviewer asked me about the British government's misquote that led readers of the sound-bite to think I advocated killing 100 million Muslims.

I told her, *"I'm so glad you're giving me the opportunity, because that is the most offensive misquote of all. It has also put my life in danger."* I continued:

> This quote, if I remember correctly, was made somewhat after a terrorist incident. It may have been the London bombings. I'm not sure. It could have been the Madrid bombings. And I was talking about what will happen if a radical Muslim nation gets nuclear material and threatens to use it against the West. I said, "Would you rather have a hundred million of them die, or a hundred million of us die?" Now, I think that's quite different than making it sound as though I just said randomly "go out and kill people."

That was not a call for serious criminal acts, or for terrorist violence. It was a call for leadership–leadership we are completely lacking in this generation–that would take the terrorist threat seriously and really deal with it militarily. It was strong and sharply worded. It was offensive to some; maybe to you, too.

But let me be clear: *it wasn't a call to some kind of violence,* nor was it a declaration of hatred toward Islam. In fact, the only way it has ever been taken as such is by people hearing agenda-driven enemies who isolate it from all context and then publish it abroad. They are the ones publishing and promoting hatred. My Muslim listeners certainly know better than Jacqui Smith does, although I probably can't say the same for Muslims who are given those quotes from my enemies in America, and now, mysteriously, in the British government.

Again, it comes down to political speech, which my enemies are trying to criminalize. They like our present multi-cultural leadership and don't want anyone to sharply criticize it. So they are trying to find ways through deception to silence me.

Nigel Sheinwald Attacks

As I've already told you, Jacqui Smith defended her actions as if she really knew something about me. This was totally false, unless she claims to have given real time and attention to *The Savage Nation* radio show and only if she's done some serious reading in my books. I am certain that she has done nothing of the kind, but still confidently has made declarations about me and what I stand for.

What should have happened, then, is that the British government should have at least had some expert on her staff who could honestly claim to have done this listening and reading. That person could have spoken with a claim to authority, and perhaps that person and I could have gone head-to-head in some media format. Of course, according to the secret documents I uncovered, it looks like their expert would have actually defended me! Remember, their primary researcher said that, "there is no evidence" to be found of Michael Savage "advocating or inciting violence,"

But no one in the Home Office seemed to show any awareness of such foundational principles of proof or evidence. I suspect this is because the only person who could claim to be such an expert, and who might still insist that I am guilty, would have been some as-yet-undisclosed, agenda-driven U.S. citizen.

To expose this person in the media would have immediately opened up his or her relationships with U.S. politicians and organizations. I suspect that would have revealed more international collusion than the Home Office wants to allow us to see.

So instead, they simply handed a fax or emailed a memo to some politico, the so-called "Sir" Nigel Sheinwald, the British Ambassador to the United States, who went on National Public Radio and attacked me as if, among all his duties and DC cocktail parties, he had taken the time to thoroughly get to know *The Savage Nation* radio show and his books.

I quote below his words about what the Home Office did, though it does lose something if you can't enjoy his snotty accent:

> The list ... released the other week by our Home Office, had about 20 people on it for the last year. So you're talking about 20 out of 30-odd million. That's a very, very small number. They're a mixture of people. They are people who have a background in religious extremism; others who have expressed extreme views in other ways. I'm sorry to say that some of the things which Mr. Savage has said, which are on the record, were, in the view of our government, likely to inflame and to cause hatred and possibly violence.

I have to say that listening to this, after I had to hire security guards due to the Home Office's libel of me, was rather hard to take. I don't care if he is a British ambassador; he's lower than a slug. *He* was the one actually doing the very thing he said I'm doing. He painted a target on my back.

To give the devil his due, it is truly amazing to see a man appear on the radio and basically admit that they pulled twenty names at random out of thirty million people, and then act like this somehow is credit to the Home Office. Brits can basically say anything on American radio, no matter how fatuous and criminal, and it always sounds like intellectual sophistication to our ears. Even so, he could only get away with it in the US on the government-controlled National Public Radio. I invited him, "Sir" or not, to come on *The Savage Nation* and debate with me. No surprise–he will not respond to my invitation.

It is difficult to even get to the bottom of the lies or misdirections that Sheinwald fit into the forty-second sound-bite quoted above. The list contains names of people who have committed murder. It contains the names of people now serving long prison sentences. It contains the name of a Hamas terrorist who killed a Jewish baby by smashing a rifle butt into her head, after shooting both of her parents. To claim this is a list of "people who have a background in religious extremism; others who have expressed extreme views in other ways," is a deception designed to rationalize the British government's injustice, including my name on the list.

As my lawyers pointed out to Hillary Clinton, Sir Sheinwald is in violation of European Union law. Furthermore, I believe it is men like him who destroyed his country in the past. Men like him have led Britain over the abyss, economically and culturally, in my opinion. I'm sure he felt no problem smearing me on NPR. It isn't just what he does, it is who he is. He is a fraud, and an empty suit.

Sir Nigel Elton Sheinwald, the current British Ambassador to the United States, was educated at Harrow County School for Boys and at Balliol College Oxford, where apparently he spent his days learning nothing. He learned nothing about the Magna Carta. He learned nothing about due process. He learned nothing about the common-law tradition of England (something about British history that is genuinely great and worth remembering and recovering). He learned nothing about free speech.

But apparently he learned how to impress himself and his parents with a snotty eunuch-like accent. You see, he was Foreign Office Press Secretary and head of the news department from 1995-1998. That means he was an expert in propaganda. That means he was an expert at dissimulating the truth. That means he was an expert in what Orwell dubbed *newspeak* in his novel, *1984.*

I may not have Sheinwald's background. Mine is ten times better than his. And I may not have the education he has. Mine is fifty times better than his. I have a *real* Ph.D. from the University of California at Berkley. He can have his groupies look it up.

Here is something else we know about Sheinwald: Sir Nigel is credited with successfully negotiating the release of fifteen Royal Navy personnel from Iran in 2007. He made a critical breakthrough in the standoff during a call with the head of Iran's supreme National Security Council, Ali Larijani.

Now, if you remember, that was an embarrassing moment in history for the Royal Navy, when sailors were kidnapped without firing a shot. The British Navy did not defend itself. A group of rag-tag Iranian sailors boarded a British ship and kidnapped these defenseless children and took them to Iran. The defenseless, socialist government of Britain did not fire a shot. The defenseless British government had to watch one of their soldiers crying on television. The defenseless British government, instead of taking action, sent Sheinwald over there to beg for their release. That's apparently something that he's good at doing with dictators–begging.

As I pointed out on the radio after first hearing his NPR interview, Sheinwald will soon be thrown out of office. They're all going to be thrown out of office very soon. The Speaker of the House of Commons resigned–the first one in 300 years, because of the level of corruption in England. Very soon, all of them will be thrown out of office. This corrupt regime is in no position to pass judgment on me. In fact, passing judgment on me was a strategy to try to make themselves look important–to appear to have moral authority. They are, in fact, proving the very opposite.

On *The Savage Nation*, I addressed Sheinwald:

> Let me tell you something. What you have done to me today is likely to cause violence against me. You have stirred up hatred amongst various groups. You have inflamed various groups against me with your big lie. So the very thing you are accusing me of, you snotty

eunuch, you are doing of course. And, you see Nigel, I don't know if you ever read the Bible at Balliol–I don't know if they still know what the Bible actually is, even though Britain was built on the Bible–there is actually a commandment which says the following, Nigel. Pay attention: "Thou shalt not bear false witness against thy neighbor." Now, the British are my neighbors. Your government has borne false witness against me. You have committed a biblical sin against me. But since we are not living in a biblical world, but a legal world, I will act accordingly.

I also read Sheinwald and his entire Labour government a quotation from Shylock in Act 3, Scene 1, in Shakespeare's *The Merchant of Venice*:

He hath disgraced me, and hindered me half a million; laughed at my losses, mocked at my gains, scorned my nation, thwarted my bargains, cooled my friends, heated mine enemies; and what's his reason? I am a Jew. Hath not a Jew eyes? Hath not a Jew hands, organs, dimensions, senses, affections, passions? Fed with the same food, hurt with the same weapons, subject to the same diseases, healed by the same means, warmed and cooled by the same winter and summer, as a Christian is? If you prick us, do we not bleed? If you tickle us, do we not laugh? If you poison us, do we not die? And if you wrong us, shall we not revenge? If we are like you in the rest, we will resemble you in that.

As you can tell, being put on that list and banned from Britain was something I took very personally. I was resolved to do all I could to completely clear my name and, whether or not I succeeded, to do everything I could do to help Jacqui Smith lose her job. In that much, I have already succeeded.

Jacqui Smith Steps Down

As I've already noted, Jacqui Smith seems to have developed this "name and shame" list as a way of compensating for, or distracting people from, her record of incompetency and corruption. Maybe if I had been over-awed by the majesty of the British Government and cooperated by keeping silent, I would have allowed her plan to work.

But that was never going to happen!

So instead of subtracting from her other problems, banning me from Britain and "naming and shaming" me became an *additional* strike against her record as Home Secretary. Within two days a British online newspaper ran the headline, **"Savaged by Shock Jock, Smith Also Faces the Sack."**[5]

> If anyone in Gordon Brown's Cabinet is having a worse week than the boss himself–disgruntled backbenchers are plotting to remove him as Labour leader, according to an exclusive report posted today by *The First Post*'s "Westminster Mole"–it is his embattled Home Secretary, Jacqui Smith. She faces a lawsuit … she faces the sack from her current job, and she's the subject of yet another allegation of questionable behavior regarding her infamous "second home."

The story goes on to suggest that Jacqui would lose her position soon after June 4, 2009. But it didn't take that long. Her resignation was announced June 2, after I was interviewed by Victoria Derbyshire that morning on a popular radio show that received a great many outraged callers who defended me against the ban. As one American headline put it, **"Don't mess with Savage! U.K. home secretary quits: Jacqui Smith banned radio talker, he sued, now she's stepping down."**[6] It wasn't a complete vindication yet, but it was still a great taste of what I hope will be better things to come.

A few weeks later, I received more good news. The woman who banned me from Britain as the Secretary of the Home Office admitted that she was not up to the challenge or prepared for the job. According to the *Daily Mail*,

> She said she was thrust into one of the biggest posts in Government without any training and called for MPs to receive help before they become ministers. She also suggested that any successes she had in her post were due to "luck" rather than skill.[7]

I'm glad Jacqui is finally admitting this. I just wish she would take me up on my offer and apologize to me about including me on her "name and shame" list.

Sadly, the Home Office and the new Secretary, while they seem to have admitted at times that the list was a bad idea, will not renounce it or end that ban on me traveling to England. So I am still waiting for justice to be done.

But I am not just waiting. I continue to bear the heavy expense of a legal representation both in the United States and in Britain. I continue to work to get full disclosure of any relevant information about how the decision was made, using the Freedom of Information Act in the U.S. and similar Freedom of Information legislation in England. I have no plans to quit this struggle. I will continue to fight the good fight until I get my name off that list, get an apology, and get compensation for all the damages and expenses that I have incurred.

And then I may go to England, for the first time in more than twenty years, with a cruise ship of thousands of Savage supporters. We will land at Southhampton. And then, triumphantly, I will give the speech of my life before Parliament–on the meaning of free speech. "God save the Queen!"

As I mentioned in the Preface, as the book goes to press I have sent a final appeal and warning to Jacqui Smith. In many ways, this letter from my lawyers was like their original letter in May. However, because Jacqui Smith was no longer the Secretary of the Home Office, "We now write you in your personal capacity." We were also able to summarize not only the false and damaging nature of her claims, but with the new secret emails and documents revealed, also show how baseless were her actions even from the perspective of her own discussions.

- We note from the "Exclusion Research Proforma (at pages 2 to 6) that it was found (at page 2) that "there is no evidence of [our client] advocating or inciting violence." Notwithstanding this information, you agreed to publish the Press Release which stated expressly that our client sought to provoke criminal acts.

- We note from an email between Home Office officials timed at 2.20 pm on 1 December 2008 (page 40) that the author of that email was of the opinion that the Home Office "could be accused of duplicity by naming our client and not other individuals on the exclusion list. Despite these concerns, you decided to name our client in the published list.

It would be wonderful if Jacqui Smith would reflect on what she has done and apologize. But to be honest, I don't think it is likely that she will.

So how did this all start? When I first heard of the British Government's actions against me, I had no idea if I would be able to win any battles in this war against censorship. If you think the past few months were easy, you would be wrong. In the next chapter I go back to the beginning of my story.

Chapter Notes

1 *The Telegraph* has a web page dedicated to this issue:http://www. telegraph.co.uk/news/newstopics/mps-expenses/

2 Kelefa Sanneh, "Party of One: Michael Savage, Unexpurgated," *The New Yorker*, August 3, 2009, 53.

3 See also Glen Owen, "US shock jock Savage targeted 'to balance least wanted list'," *The Daily Mail*, July 25, 2009, http://www.dailymail.co.uk/news/article-1202169/US-shock-jock-Savage-targeted-balance-wanted-list.html (Last viewed July 25, 2009).

4 At the time of this writing you can listen to the interview as accompanying audio with the story, "Banned 'shock jock' fights back," *BBC News*, June 2, 2009, http://news.bbc.co.uk/2/hi/uk_news/8079111.stm (Last viewed on August 8, 2009). I replayed the interview on my show; an audio was made by someone and posted on http://www.youtube.com/watch?v=hKg5eXy_5DY

5 Lara Ellington-Brown, *The First Post*, May 7, 2009, http://www. thefirstpost.co.uk/47448,news,savaged-by-shock-jock-jacqui-smith-also-faces-the-sack (Last viewed on July 25, 2009).

6 *World Net Daily*, June 2, 2009, Last viewed July 25, 2009. http://www. wnd.com/index.php?fa=PAGE.view&pageId=99917

7 Daniel Martin, "Jacqui Smith: I'd never run a thing before the Home Office," *Daily Mail*, July 17, 2009, http://www.dailymail.co.uk/news/article-1200108/Jacqui-Smith-admits-wasnt-Home-Secretary.html (Last viewed July 17, 2009).

2

The Day of Defamation

When you approach a set of traffic lights, you know to slow down on a yellow light, to stop on a red light, or keep going on a green light. Signs announce the speed limit.

But what if you are on the autobahn in Germany where there are no speed limits and no traffic lights? You drive as fast as you dare, limited only by your car's performance capabilities, your nerves, and your driving skills. As one of America's blunt talk radio hosts, I have spoken at maximum speeds. For fifteen years I have attempted to speak the truth about where politicians are taking us, without posted limits–save a few, such as "We do not kill in talk radio," or "We do not attack the defenseless." I have attracted an increasingly large and loyal following to my broadcasts, estimated to be eight to ten million regular weekly listeners.

Never have I seen a "traffic light" or a "road sign" warning me to slow down or stop. When my words have shocked powerful lobbying groups, I paid dearly, once losing a major television talk show and also some advertisers. In some cases my words were twisted by my political opponents. But whenever clear warning signs were posted, I followed the rules, adjusting my words but not my meaning.

Yet without warning, out of the atmosphere it seemed, the British Government made up their own imaginary rules of acceptable speech. And without any warning they condemned an innocent, honest man. This book is an attempt to set the record straight and clear my name.

I remember the 1960's when true liberals used to say, "I may disagree with you, but I would fight to the death for your right to say it." When have you last heard a liberal use that slogan in response to conservative talk radio? I don't hear liberals saying that anymore. What I hear instead is, "they are threats to national security" as was stated by Democrat Congressman Maurice Hinchey of New York. Others say they only want "fairness." Feinstein, Kerry and Durbin are the leading voices for government censorship. Is this liberalism? We cannot permit a few, small minded martinets to deny us our freedom of speech.

Where are the true good liberals? Radio is in a more perilous state today than in its entire history. In South America, the dictator Hugo Chavez closed down opposition TV stations. "Well," you say, "that can't happen here." What do you mean, it can't happen here? A bill is circulating in Congress to bring back the so called Fairness Doctrine.

This would amount to government control over political views stated on the public airwaves. Michael Savage will no longer be able to speak freely. Is that any different than Chavez closing down a TV station? Is that not a dictatorship of ideas? Of course it is. It's just that we use fancy rhetoric in this country as opposed to police power. But make no mistake about it—the Fairness Doctrine is censorship and has no place in the United States of America.

For example, Al Gore, in my opinion, lies when he preaches that all scientists now agree that global warming is caused by human activity. If I refute Gore's lies on the airwaves by quoting numerous prominent scientists who refute Gore's hysterical con, I am using the freedom of speech granted to us by the United States Constitution. Some radical environmental folks want to make it a crime to deny global warming. Such refutations as mine and those of prominent scientists would be banished from the discussion.

Ahmadinejad, the new Hitler of our time and so-called president of Iran, has declared his desire to create a new holocaust against the Jews. And yet we see prominent lawyers and journalists in our own country—some of Jewish descent—denying the Islamofascist connection. Worse yet, they defend Islamic murderers, in Guantanamo and elsewhere, who would gladly cut their throats or decapitate them while chanting to Allah. Out of fear of offending the SS of today, they refuse to talk about the codification of hatred for Jews, Israel, the United States, and our way of life.

Why do these intellectuals deny their own freedom of speech to defend the freedom to preach hatred by their enemies? Daniel Pearl, the journalist from the *Wall Street Journal* who was executed and decapitated by the Islamofascists, was forced to say, "I am a Jew, my mother was a Jew," before Islamic murderers cut off his head while chanting to Allah. Yet that was never played on the major media. If I were to play Daniel Pearl's blood curdling screams as he is dying, as his head is being severed, would the government require me to play the Islamofascist view, that all Jews are evil? Doesn't the Fairness Doctrine say that opposing views must be heard?

I want to define satire, ridicule, and sarcasm for those of us who love talk radio. *Satire* is the use of irony, sarcasm, ridicule or the like in exposing, denouncing or deriding vice, folly, etc. What is *ridicule?* We use it on talk radio all the time if we know how. It is speech or action intended to cause contemptuous laughter, at a person or thing. Derision, my friends, is ridicule. That's part of freedom of speech. And finally, sarcasm should be used all the time if you know how to do it. What is *sarcasm?* Harsh or bitter derision or irony, a sharply ironical taunt, a sneering or cutting remark. That's freedom of speech, my friends.

When I offend doctrinaire knee-jerk Republicans by pointing out there are now more contractors than U.S. soldiers in Iraq, whose freedom am I denying? The freedom of the military-industrial complex to rob the public? The freedom of those who refuse to either win definitively or leave? Eisenhower warned us, "Beware the military-industrial complex." When I play that on my show as I have repeatedly, who am I criticizing: Democrats or Republicans? I'll let you decide. When I state that our Army and Marine heroes are being sent in to fight door-to-door, to suffer and die, and then given court-martials if they do their job just a little too well, whose freedoms am I denying?

President Bush said that he will not have politicians telling our generals how to conduct a war. I wonder: *Is he not a politician telling generals how to conduct a war?* No war has ever been conducted like this. And when I call illegal aliens "invaders" who must be deported, and I present the social and fiscal drain of this invading army, whose freedoms am I denying? Who am I offending? The doctrinaire knee-jerk Republicans or the Democrats? Probably both.

When I support my position for borders, language, and culture, do I deny my fellow citizens their right to redress their grievances to a government all too eager to continue flooding our nation with cheap laborers? When I present the fact that about 30% of all prisoners are illegal aliens, do I deny or do I grant my fellow U.S. citizens their right to speak freely through me, a talk show host? When I detail the epidemic of drunk driving and vehicular homicides being inflicted on this country by brazen illegal aliens, who are deported only to return and drive drunk again, drive and kill again, I surely do not deny my fellow Americans their freedom of speech or right to redress their grievances, do I? So whose rights am I offending? Certain special interests, I would assume.

If these and other like opinions were mine alone, I would not have risen to the position I now enjoy in the world of the spoken and written word. Because of my radio program, I am the voice of the voiceless, those who have been marginalized and silenced by the lack of balance in the media. The limited exception is conservative talk radio, the most vulnerable medium, which is under attack by those who would ban free speech that they disagree with. There are those who want to achieve the same ends as in a dictatorship, as with Hugo Chavez in Venezuela. Their goal is total control of speech, and the end of freedom.

America is a nation of strong opinion. Our government has no inherent right to limit conservative voices they cannot refute through argument. Moreover, should the Democrats revive the "Fairness Doctrine," will I be given access to the evening news on ABC, CBS, or NBC to give my "opposing views"? Who will determine what is "balanced" and what is "fair?" This doctrine is long dead and must remain in the ashcan of broadcast history.

To conservatives, Senator Dick Durbin's remarks comparing our own troops to Nazi storm troopers were fighting words. Should he be thrown out of the Senate, banned from Britain, or barred from Camp Pendleton? It won't happen. Not because his words are not offensive to every military person who served our nation, but because he is a member of the ruling authority in today's leftist America. What offends is not about right or wrong, but whose "ox is gored" or who is in power.

The same is true of Senator Chris Dodd, who said that Bush should be tried for war crimes because we did the same to the Nazis. So Bush, according to Dodd, is comparable to the Nazis. For conservatives, this was totally unwarranted and offensive.

This is why we have and enjoy the First Amendment! The Founding Fathers foresaw how "power corrupts," and how "absolute power corrupts absolutely."

They foresaw how powerful interests would try to kill freedom of speech to preserve their absolute power.

What Happened To Me

We the citizens of the United States live in some very interesting times, especially since November 2008 when this country took a definite turn for the worse.

"May you live in interesting times" is supposedly a Chinese curse, though no one has found the Chinese original. A speaker in 1939 claimed that a similar curse had been used, "May you live in an interesting age." He said that Neville Chamberlain's step-brother, Austen, had claimed to have heard of the phrase from a Chinese diplomat.[1] I find that ironic since Neville Chamberlain himself lived in and even helped bring about some "interesting times."

I'm not happy that we live in interesting times. But as a radio host my job is to talk about them, explain them, predict them, and beg the public to avoid them. This is what I do on *The Savage Nation*, the third most popular talk radio show in the US.

What took me completely by surprise was that my "interesting times" would not simply be the ones I experienced with all other Americans. On May 5, 2009, I received the beginning of my own special interesting times. According to one source, "May you live in interesting times," is related to another, more severe, curse: "May you come to the attention of those in authority." There is no source listed for this connection, but it seems right to me, based on personal experience. On that day, I discovered I had come to the attention of someone in authority, and it was truly a curse.

No one in authority had warned me. No one in authority asked me any questions or summoned me to answer questions. No one sent me notice that I was viewed as a threat to the peace. I found out through the news like everyone else.

I awoke around seven that morning and turned on my computer to check out the news. When I went to the *Drudge Report,* there it was right at the top of the page:

"RADIO HOST MICHAEL SAVAGE BANNED FROM UK FOR 'EXTREME VIEWS'... DETAILS..." There was a link to the British website, *The Independent.*

The headline ran, **"Named and Shamed: The 16 Barred from the UK."** Before one could even read the text, the first thing that one saw was a large picture of my own face right beside the text.

I was totally shocked by what I saw. In fact, I thought I had to be seeing things. I simply couldn't believe it. Before following the link from the *Drudge Report,* I thought it must be some kind of joke, or some rumor perpetrated by enemies of the show. But I found that sure enough, reputable newspapers in England had reported that the British Home Office, the equivalent of our State Department, had placed me on a list of those who are prohibited from entering the country.

Here is what the website of the British Home Office said:

> Individuals banned from the UK for stirring-up hatred have been named and shamed for the first time, the Home Secretary announced today. The list covers people excluded from the United Kingdom for fostering extremism or hatred between October 2008 and March 2009.

And there was my name on the list:

> **Michael Savage:** Controversial daily radio host. Considered to be engaging in unacceptable behavior by seeking to provoke others to serious criminal acts and fostering hatred which might lead to inter-community violence.

The accusation that I was "fostering hatred" was paranoid and so subjective that it basically could be used to marginalize anyone who expressed any strong viewpoint. But the claim that I was "seeking to provoke others to serious criminal acts" was even more serious. It was a totally false statement.

I instinctively tried to find the funny side to what I was reading. It did seem humorous that the Home Office was acting like I had a burning desire to visit their country (though I am a life-long Anglophile). The first thought I had was, "Darn, there goes the summer trip to receive their fine dental care." My second thought was "Darn, I'll have to give up my summer trip where I was going to do a tour of British restaurants for their famous cuisine."

But then I realized that this was no joke. I ran down the names of others who had been placed on the list and was instantly outraged. Here is a small portion of the list.

> **Artur Ryno** and **Pavel Skachevsky**: Leaders of a violent gang that beat migrants and posted films of their attacks on the Internet. Considered to be engaging in unacceptable behavior by fomenting serious criminal activity and seeking to provoke others to serious criminal acts.

There is that word, "considered," again. But in this case the claims about that behavior were much more specific and serious.

> **Abdullah Qadri Al Ahdal**: Preacher. Considered to be engaging in unacceptable behavior by seeking to foment, justify or glorify terrorist violence in furtherance of particular beliefs and fostering hatred which might lead to inter-community violence.

I, on the other hand, have always opposed terrorist violence. "So why am I, Michael Savage, listed with these people?" I wondered.

> **Yunis Al Astal**: Preacher. Considered to be engaging in unacceptable behavior by seeking to foment, justify or glorify terrorist violence in furtherance of particular beliefs and to provoke others to terrorist acts.

> **Wadgy Abd El Hamied Mohamed Ghoneim**: A prolific speaker and writer. Considered to be engaging in unacceptable behavior by seeking to foment, justify or glorify terrorist violence in furtherance of particular beliefs and to provoke others to commit terrorist acts.

> **Abdul Ali Musa**: Considered to be engaging in unacceptable behavior by fomenting and glorifying terrorist violence in furtherance of his particular beliefs and seeking to provoke others to terrorist acts.

> **Samir Al Quntar**: Spent three decades in prison for killing four soldiers and a four-year-old girl. Considered to be engaging in

unacceptable behavior by seeking to foment, justify or glorify terrorist violence in furtherance of particular beliefs and to provoke others to terrorist acts.

It was absolutely unbelievable! I had been placed on a list with madmen who had murdered Jewish children by bashing their skulls in with rifle butts. I was on the list with Islamofascists who had threatened the violent overthrow of the British government. I was on a list with violent Nazi skinheads who were serving ten-year sentences for murder in Russia.

This was pure insanity. How can they put Michael Savage in the same league with mass murderers when I have never avowed violence? If I had ever avowed violence I would not be on the radio. I would not have lasted fifteen minutes, let alone fifteen years. The (US) FCC would have kicked me off the air immediately. In fact, my opinions are more in keeping with the mainstream of America than some people would like to believe. But even if my opinions are wildly unpopular, why should that be of any concern to the British government or any other government claiming to be a democracy? Since there is no basis for accusing me of promoting violence, the only excuse left for barring me is that I have said things that someone important in the British government doesn't like. Or perhaps I have said something in a way that someone in the British government doesn't like. So what? The whole point of the rights guaranteed by the First Amendment is to protect offensive speech, not polite speech.

Even though the British do not officially have a First Amendment explicitly enshrined in law, to the extent that they claim to have political freedom as a representative democracy, they have to allow people to state their opinions. Otherwise, the government could prevent others from running for office or prevent the people from voting for them. Without freedom of speech and freedom of the press, democracy is a sham.

To put the Home Office's list in some context, consider some people who are permitted to reside and be protected in Britain:[2]

Abu Qatada:

This man is in jail and fighting extradition to Jordan on charges of terrorism. He is Osama Bin Laden's top man in the UK.

Learco Chindamo:
This Italian is staying in Britain because deporting him would violate his human right to a family life. Murdered a school headmaster in 1995.

Ahsan Sabri:
This Pakistani entered Britain illegally and married a British woman. It is now illegal to deport this illegal immigrant due to his alleged human right to a family life. He killed a young writer by running into her at sixty miles per hour in a car that he drove–despite having neither a driver's license nor insurance.

Caliph Ali Asmar:
This Iraqi Kurd who came to Britain seeking asylum is now imprisoned for life since he raped a woman and knifed a rival. Before that crime he was sentenced to two years for "unlawful wounding," but was released and allowed to stay in the UK after only eight months.

Paul Gadd:
Now going by the stage name, "Gary Glitter," former pop star Gadd spent almost three years in a Vietnam prison for sex crimes he committed with two young girls. He got to return to Britain in August 2007, even though he has also served a two-month sentence for possession of child porn in 1999.

Dr Philip Nitschke:
Called "Dr. Death," this hardcore euthanasia advocate won his nickname by bringing suicide workshops to the United Kingdom. In Australia, he is known to have assisted four people commit suicide. He was permitted to come and teach in England even though assisted suicide is supposed to be illegal, carrying a fourteen-year prison term as the maximum punishment.

So I ask you this: while these people cannot be taken from England, is Michael Savage really too dangerous to be let in?

Do I Have a Right to Be Shocked?

Voltaire's viewpoint has been enshrined not only in the United States, but internationally as well. The United Nations Universal Declaration of Human Rights states in Articles 18 and 19:

> Everyone has the right to freedom of thought, conscience and religion; this right includes freedom to change his religion or belief, and freedom, either alone or in community with others and in public or private, to manifest his religion or belief in teaching, practice, worship and observance.

> Everyone has the right to freedom of opinion and expression; this right includes freedom to hold opinions without interference and to seek, receive and impart information and ideas through any media and regardless of frontiers.

Furthermore, that same Declaration also says, *"No one shall be subjected to arbitrary interference with his privacy, family, home or correspondence, nor to attacks upon his honor and reputation. Everyone has the right to the protection of the law against such interference or attacks"* (Article 12).

Also, Article 7 is very relevant: *"All are equal before the law and are entitled without any discrimination to equal protection of the law. All are entitled to equal protection against any discrimination in violation of this Declaration and against any incitement to such discrimination"* (emphasis added). Considering that I was made the object of an official government action without any recourse to the law, much less due process, the next article may also be relevant. *"Everyone has the right to an effective remedy by the competent national tribunals for acts violating the fundamental rights granted him by the constitution or by law."*

I'm tempted to say the next article, Article Nine, should apply because being banned from a country seems a great deal like exile: *"No one shall be subjected to arbitrary arrest, detention or exile."*

Article Ten is even more appropriate: *"Everyone is entitled in full equality to a fair and public hearing by an independent and impartial tribunal, in the determination of his rights and obligations and of any criminal charge against him."*

You should know, if you don't already, that I'm not a great fan of the United Nations. The "right" to a standard of living is also found in these Articles, for example, and I doubt such a right can be guaranteed by governments, nor should it be. But these articles do provide some initial confirmation that expecting the right to political free speech is not a privilege that is supposed to be restricted to United States citizens. To be permitted to speak freely without government interference, and to have recourse to the law when accused of wrongdoing, are pretty basic rights that are uncontroversial in most Western, open, societies.

Or, at least, they used to be and they should be.

The fact of the matter is that it is an obvious assault on me, on my reputation and good name, to put me on a list with murderers and terrorists. I have not promoted criminal acts–serious or otherwise. Period. I do not advocate violence, but I do oppose terrorism. I have not been convicted of any criminal wrongdoing in any court. In fact, I've never been accused of any criminal wrongdoing in any court. I have been on the air a decade and a half and no one has even accused me of causing violence.

Furthermore, the United States and Britain have enjoyed a long-standing, close relationship, which may not be the case with some of the other people on the banned list. It makes no sense that Britain would unilaterally ban an American from her land. What has happened to me is completely at odds with that legacy.

Sitting at my computer, and looking at the headlines that day, I realized that somehow none of these considerations mattered. Evidently, Voltaire's attitude was not present in the British government, nor does the United Nation's Universal Declaration of Human Rights hold much weight. The long tradition of peace and travel between our two countries no longer applies to me.

I tried to wrap my mind around what was being done to me. *My views are held by tens of millions of people who listen to my program in the United States, and I'm certain by millions more who don't listen to me,* I thought.

Did the Home Office have any intention of acting with principled consistency in accordance with their treatment of me? Would they ban my listeners from going to their wonderful nation as well? Would my dog, Teddy, the ten pound poodle, also be banned if I appeared at Heathrow with him? I wondered if he would be considered a potential threat, and if the Home Office would be concerned that he might incite inter-kennel anxiety, or something like that.

The truth was, I hadn't planned on going to England, and I hadn't been there in over twenty-five years. But I couldn't just leave it at that. This issue was more important than my convenience. A precedent was being set here. A government was testing the waters in banning political speech. *Today it's me,* I thought, *but tomorrow it will be someone else.*

I had to fight back.

As a start, I called for all eight to ten million of my listeners to cancel their visits to England over the coming year. I decided to ask them to stop buying goods that come out of the United Kingdom. I decided to demonstrate the muscle and the power of *The Savage Nation.* How can I do otherwise? I have no recourse to any British court until after the damage is done (and then I only have the private courts to use at my own expense). Tragically, there was never a hearing when I could learn of (let alone respond to) the charges against me in advance. I have to use what powers I have.

Conservatives travel. Conservatives spend money. Conservatives buy beer. Conservatives buy machinery. Conservatives buy…everything. Now I am a great supporter of things English, but until my name is taken off that list, I will continue encouraging my listeners to avoid traveling to England and buying English products.

The good new is, we are making a difference! One great conservative listener, who owns a bakery operation, wrote to inform me what he was doing about the treatment I am receiving from Britain. He not only shows the economic power of *The Savage Nation,* but also represents in many ways what *The Savage Nation* is all about. I love what he wrote. Here are some major portions of his letter to me:

> *Dear Michael,*
>
> *I am a 52-year-old first generation Armenian American. Similar to your background, mine was also unusual and shaped the nature of my destiny and insight into the world. My grandparents fled their home in the Hatay region of Turkey, during the Genocide, with only their lives.*

They settled in Jerusalem where both of my parents were born. God had blessed my grandfather, father, and family. Starting with nothing, through great hardship and tenacity, they built a prosperous business.

My father, always with great foresight, was fed up with the fighting which led up to the partition of Palestine and the formation of Israel. Their business was at the center of a "no man's land." They were fired upon from both sides. We believe the formation of Israel was a fulfillment of Bible prophecy, however, being Armenian, this was not our fight.

Ultimately, my father dreamed to come to this great country and, in 1948, he moved with his new wife and baby. He knew this nation was unique and special.

My father started at least a dozen businesses, not all successful, all the while teaching my brothers and me what it took to be an entrepreneur and build a business. We struggled very much.

My father, brother, and I started a bakery in 1978 with meager resources. Being machine designer/builders, we designed and hand-built a unique high speed process for Pita, Flatbread, and Pizza crust. The company's history was much like your own, filled with brutal events of survival. I believe it was the prophetic prayers of my grandmother that preserved us. We now, by God's grace, are the industry leader.

Even though I have experienced great personal success, the warnings of my grandfather and father (both passed away in 1987 and 1993, respectively) grip my mind. My father was proud of this country but constantly feared the poisons of the radical left. He would often comment, "This country will lose its freedom because people don't know the value of what they have."

My grandfather, in the sixties, was horrified to see some of the most radical Muslims he knew from the old country now living here. Shocked that such people would be permitted to enter the country, he would say,

"Some day these types of people will burn this country. We will be like sheep for the slaughter."

I and my family have worked so hard to build a future. I, like yourself, fear for my family's future. I see what is rapidly coming. God is our only hope!

Michael, God put you in the place you are in for a reason, much like he put Queen Esther in the court of Xerxes to save his people from Haman. I know he has a plan for you, and I will continue to pray that he strengthens you and restores the courage that he has blessed you with. You may not believe it, but you are a part of God's plan. Your boldness, fearlessness, and righteous indignation is unmatched.

Michael, I beg you not to give up your fight. I have been listening for nearly 6 years. I don't miss a word of your show. I quote you constantly throughout the day. They call me "Sam Savage." Your fight is my fight!

We recently purchased and installed several freezing systems from the UK at a cost of approximately five million dollars. I called the British Council General in L.A. and left word that we will no longer buy them in the future. We will also cancel our plans to buy the first of four packaging systems at 2.2 million dollars each from a British company, and will choose otherwise.

What a brilliant letter. And you can't overlook one of his many profound statements: *"This country will lose its freedom because people don't know the value of what they have."* In addition to his boycott of Britain, this dear listener contributed ten thousand dollars to my legal defense fund. What a godly and patriotic American.

Talk Radio and the Nature of Free Speech

At this point, let me remind you of two important points to keep in mind as you think about these issues. First of all, (as I mentioned above) there has been quite a lot of noise recently about curbing free speech in the case of Talk Radio.

As reported on the Real Clear Politics blog, the Speaker of the House, Nancy Pelosi, does not hide her desire to find a tool to censor the radio:

> When asked this week if she supported revival of the Fairness Doctrine, Pelosi answered, reportedly without hesitation: "Yes." In 2007, according to the conservative American Spectator magazine, a Pelosi adviser had said, "Conservative radio is a huge threat and political advantage for Republicans, and we have had to find a way to limit it."[3]

What this has to do with the actions of the Home Office, if anything, is something I will discuss later on in this book. But the point for now is that there is a great deal at stake in the minds of some politicians. I was not selected at random. I was selected precisely because I am a member of a class—a class made up of conservative radio talk show hosts—that is considered a problem to a powerful group of people in politics.

People have free speech *when they know that they can say what they believe without fearing government reprisals.* When politicians work to punish people for what they say, and when they single out a person in order to intimidate others, that government is not allowing freedom of speech and of the press. If citizens have to fear how the government might inflict payback on them for what they say, then their speech is effectively being censored.

Who Is Jacqui Smith?

The real question that bothered me was this: Who put this list together? And who was out to get me?

According to the Home Office, there were another six names of people who were banned from the country whose names they refused even to disclose. Was Kim Jong-Il on that list because he allegedly killed over one million of his own fellow countrymen? Was Hugo Chavez on that list of banned people in England because he has driven at least fifteen to twenty thousand Jews out of his own nation because of his hate talk? This was crazy.

I had to find out more about who was responsible for dragging my good name through the mud. Who in the British government put this list together?

Who in all England could claim to put me in the same category as these demons? My show is not even broadcast in England. What shows had they heard that led them to believe that I had advocated murder?

It was clear to me that the person or persons responsible knew nothing about my program, and I had been singled out simply for political purposes. I was about to find out that, just as the Neo-Marxists in this country use their political offices to shower unreasoned hatred upon their enemies, so do the members of the leftist Labour Party in the United Kingdom. The only difference is that we have a First Amendment and they don't. But as I have pointed out, this should not make that much difference regarding political speech. The United Kingdom, as a society that has elections for rulers, ought to allow freedom of expression of political beliefs.

I soon found out the name I was seeking: Jacqui Smith, the British Home Secretary, an equivalent position to the US Secretary of State. Since it would take me months and a lot of money spent on top lawyers to reveal the secret documents showing that the decision to ban me went up even to the Prime Minister, her name was the only one available to me on that first day.

Let me tell you something about this woman who carried out the government's desires and may well have taken a fall for her superiors. Jacqui Smith was born in Worcestershire. She studied at Oxford and later became a school teacher and began molding the minds of British schoolchildren. Jacqui Smith was eventually chosen to run for Parliament for the Labour Party from an all-female shortlist. So Smith was a product of British affirmative action. This party practice of excluding men from running for certain seats was ruled illegal in 1996 because it violated England's own sex discrimination laws. Despite the ruling, Smith stayed in place as a candidate for the following year's race. Elected in 1997, she had the smallest majority of any member of the Cabinet. (She won her last election by 1,948 votes.) In 2003, she was appointed deputy Minister for Women.

In 2007, Smith was appointed as Home Secretary, which combines the offices of Secretary of State and Homeland Security Secretary in the US. In 2008, she announced sweeping new police powers. She has pushed for legislation mandating a National Identity Card for all Britons, for which biometric fingerprints, DNA samples, and photographs would be required. By 2009, a poll of Labour

Party members showed that Smith was the least popular member of the government. She only had a fifty-six-percent approval rating.

Additionally, Smith was investigated for inappropriate expenses she claimed as a member of the British Parliament. She was caught claiming a total of 116,000 pounds in expenses for her sister's house in London even though she had claimed a different house as her primary home. And just two months before she banned me from Britain for "engaging in unacceptable behavior," it was discovered she had claimed the cost of pornographic films viewed by her husband, Richard Timney, as an expense as a Member of Parliament. The movies were "By Special Request" and "Raw Meat 3." Prime Minister Gordon Brown said she had done nothing wrong. No wonder she loyally did his will.

Despite Jacqui Smith's widespread unpopularity, "a series of angry letters published in the *Redditch Advertiser* in Worcestershire," appeared in late 2008, "attacking the Tories over schools and backing Ms Smith's controversial identity-cards plan."[4] But it turned out that the letter writer was none other than her husband, Mr. Timney, and that he was even paid a great deal of government money to be her advisor. Not surprisingly, he didn't identify himself in these letters so that no one would realize his relationship to the politician he was defending.

Footage can be found on the internet of Jacqui Smith wearing a hajib and speaking with traditional Muslim women. Presumably she is wearing the garment to show her respect for Muslims and assure the women that she is open and embracing. If these women read at all, they must now know about "Raw Meat 3." I somehow doubt there were many women wearing a hajib in that movie.

Does Ms. Smith think she is capable of winning the respect of any traditionalist believers in any religion by such gimmicks when everyone knows she has no such commitments? She actually made headlines by wearing especially low-cut dresses and tops and revealing ample cleavage in Parliament. And she even admitted it was probably not appropriate or helpful to the other MPs to get work done.

A more telling problem she had during her tenure, I later learned, was the discovery that the Home Office could not follow the law regarding immigration. Problems dogged her even though her department was in charge of bringing in a new immigration points system in 2008 to limit the number of migrants who can come to work in the UK from outside Europe.

- In May 2006 five illegal immigrants were arrested after working as cleaners at the Home office. They were working for a firm contracted by the UK Immigration and Nationality Directorate in central London.

- In December 2007 it was uncovered that an illegal immigrant was working on front desk at Home Office in Whitehall, checking people's passes.

- Also in 2007 it was revealed that 11,000 workers had been given licenses for security posts by the Security Industry Authority, even though they did not have the right to work in the UK.

- 8,000 workers had acquired National Insurance numbers.

- One of these workers had been taking care of the Prime Minister's car.

- In February 2008, an illegal immigrant was found to have been working as a cleaner in the House of Commons.

- When asked if she could guarantee there no illegal immigrants working at the Home Office, she said: "No, of course I can't. I am not going to give people reassurances and guarantees that I cannot deliver."[5]

To say the least, she didn't do a good job on the issue of illegal immigration! Furthermore, this is an issue that shows that her mind and heart are pretty much opposed, not only to the laws of her own land, but to my own values and beliefs. Of course, she didn't ban the UK law on immigration from entering her country. She banned me and put me in league with terrorists and killers. She placed me, an innocent man, in the same group as those convicted in court of heinous crimes.

Was this personal, Jacqui? Looks like it.

Reading about her on that fateful day, not realizing how high up the corruption went, I decided that Jacqui Smith owed me an apology and needed to take my name off this list. If she did not do this, I was going to sue her personally as a private citizen once she left office. I became committed to fighting her false and defamatory accusations until my last day on Earth.

Something is wrong with this picture. I am pretty confident that Jacqui Smith has never listened to my show, nor read any of my writings. I don't know why she doesn't look at some of my books, read them for herself, and see if they pose a threat to safety or order or see if they promote "intercommunity tension."

"Intercommunity tension" is an interesting phrase. I would think that Jacqui Smith is promoting more "intercommunity tension" with this ban than I ever could. The fact of the matter is, she is a very, very strange woman.

She seems to have banned me from entering the United Kingdom based on my political viewpoints—specifically due to my opposition to the global domination of Islamic Sharia law. I guess it puts me in the same company as Winston Churchill, and I suspect it also puts Prime Minister Gordon Brown in the same company as Neville Chamberlain.

If you've listened to even one of my shows, you know that I'm an ardent advocate for liberty and freedom. I received the *Talkers Magazine* Freedom of Speech Award in 2007. Precisely because I love liberty and freedom, I am, consequently, a leading opponent of global Islamofascism.

From Churchill to the Charlatans

There was a time when Britain stood for liberty and freedom by opposing fascism and tyranny. Those days seem to be long gone. Rather than remembering the best of their traditions, the British seem content to relive the career of Neville Chamberlain.

In another era, opponents of a different kind of fascism faced challenges from the British government as well—in the England of the 1930s, as the tide of fascism was rising higher and higher across Europe. But a vast majority of the British political establishment viewed Adolf Hitler as someone to be tolerated and appeased rather than opposed outright.

England was a nation devastated by World War I. It had lost the courage for another fight. Hitler readily took advantage of this fact as he expanded the German military and broke restrictions placed on his nation after the Great War. Then he began to dismantle Europe one piece at a time, in the name of gaining more living space, or *"lebensraum,"* for the German people. One of the few British voices that stood in clear opposition to Hitler was that of Winston Churchill.

Churchill warned that Hitler was not a man who could be trusted or appeased. He warned that England would one day have its final reckoning with this dictator. He warned the British people and the rest of Europe of the coming storm. But small-minded bureaucrats stood in his way at every turn. He was restricted by the British Broadcasting Corporation, who refused on many instances to give him time in order to air his views. Virtually banned from the air-waves, England went on in a delusional state of mind believing that it could make a deal with the devil.

Most Britons thought that all Hitler needed was just one more piece of land to satisfy him. They refused to come to terms with his psychopathic state of mind. And so it was that the Rhineland fell. Austria fell. Czechoslovakia fell. And then finally Poland fell. And it was only with this last conquest by Hitler that the people of Britain awoke. But by this time it was almost too late.

They realized that Prime Minister Neville Chamberlain, who had signed a peace accord with Hitler at Munich only to see Hitler roll his Blitzkrieg into yet another country, had been dangerously naïve. Wanting to assure Britain that they lived in "uninteresting times," he had brought about the very opposite.

So at last Britain turned to Churchill for leadership and made him Prime Minister. How many millions of lives could have been spared had the petty martinets of England allowed Churchill to speak? How many concentration camps could have been closed before they did their deadly work had Churchill's voice been heard? How much sooner might Germany and Hitler have been defeated and tyranny stopped around the world if the same kind of brainless bureaucrat we have in the British Labour Party today had been ousted before he had a chance to silence the voice of reason?

Well, sadly, here we are again.

This is the world that we have inherited. It's the world of Humpty Dumpty. It's a world that's been turned upside down. And perhaps some of you readers who identify yourselves as liberals will finally come to understand the danger you yourselves are in. My concern here is not only Britain, but primarily about what this does here in America. My concern is whether or not liberals and others will finally awaken to what is going on around them. Today it's me, but tomorrow it will be another conservative. And then the liberals will be silenced. You can count on it. If I can be summarily condemned by government action, then so can anyone, anytime they say or write something that someone in government does not like.

The fact of the matter is that we have seen an unprecedented power-grab in recent history. We have seen the current Obama administration take ownership of huge companies like General Motors–companies that were once the domain of the private sector. With government ownership come new levels of government control. It should not surprise us if we also then see new levels of government interference in free speech. Winston Churchill saw it coming. As we saw earlier in Chapter 1 in my letter to the Prime Minister, he knew socialism would mean the government could no longer tolerate free speech and would need a "Gestapo" to regulate people.

So if we believe Churchill, we should not be surprised if a government, when it is growing in power over the economy and is taking ownership of companies, starts disallowing *"free, sharp, or violently worded expressions of public discontent."* Today, Churchill's prediction seems quite prophetic for both sides of the Atlantic.

I have already mentioned that Democrats support the Fairness Doctrine in order to "deal with" talk radio. Other supporters include Senator Debbie Stabenow (MI), Senator Tom Harkin (IA), and Congressman Dennis Kucinich (OH). Congressman Maurice Hinchey (NY), Congressman Peter DeFazio (OR) and other Democrats have been sponsors of a bill that would reinstate the Fairness Doctrine. Al Gore has also come out for it. Some Republicans want it, too. Many have been told to expect a frontal assault on talk radio. Others have laughed this off, pointing out that the Obama Administration has said they are not interested in re-establishing the Fairness Doctrine. But if you expect a frontal assault, you are probably not going to be prepared for the real strategy that politicians will use–and are using already–even in the US, as we will see. Obama's Administration is much too clever to straightforwardly impose the Fairness Doctrine. They would never institute such a thing outright, because people would then see them for what they are. Instead, they're doing it in the way that the British government has done it.

Am I suggesting that the Obama administration is complicit in the British government's banning debacle? Yes, it's quite possible—no, *probable*—that this is coming from somebody in the United States government, rather than from England itself. That is the art of war, my friends. Make no mistake about it; we are facing an enemy that we have never faced in this nation before. Sun Tzu knew what the art of war was. And so do those that put this unknown Senator in the White House, a man with no experience whatsoever—a man who is now running the banks, financial institutions, automobile companies, and God knows whatever else tomorrow. At the moment, I have no way of knowing anything with certainty, but, as I will discuss in a later chapter, I think it is entirely possible that someone connected with Obama is behind this action by the British Government.

Wherever this attack came from, another question that nagged on me that day was, what recourse did I have against this British Home Office verdict and punishment?

I did see a glimmer of hope. As I've mentioned, we in America are protected by the First Amendment; in Britain they are not. And while they don't have such protections in England, there's something there that is in my favor. Defamation suits in America are very difficult to win.

On the other hand, it's much easier to win a defamation lawsuit against a citizen in England. Their laws are totally different when it comes to defamation. Do you think this woman has defamed me by linking me with murderers? Do you think this woman has defamed me by putting me on a list of banned individuals for my thoughts and my speech, as opposed to my actions?

Moreover, I've been endangered by this lunatic. She has painted a target on my back by linking me with terrorists and convicts who are in prison for killing people. Does she not think this will bring harm to me, and if she does, will she pay for it? I will let history and the British courts decide.

But that day on my radio show, I held out an opportunity to Jacqui Smith. I told her that she had a chance, right then, to do right by me. I said,

> If she will send a letter of apology to Michael Savage saying she was
> misinformed, if she will remove my name from this list of individ-
> uals, I will consider removing my threat of a lawsuit. If not, I will

sue her for defamation. According to every poll I've seen, she will be thrown out of office quite soon.[6] And if so, I will sue her as a private citizen. I will not stop until I am in a court of law, in England, and Home Secretary, Jacqui Smith, has to face me and has to answer for what she has done to my reputation and my name. I have spent my entire life building my reputation. I have earned degrees from great universities. I have written over twenty-five books that have been published. I have saved many, many plants in rain forests and I will not have some twit in the British government defame my name. Her name will be darkened, not mine! I am a national treasure; she is a national disgrace!

Chapter Notes

[1] Coudert, Frederic R. (May 1939). *"Preparedness and Foreign Policy: Introduction"*. Proceedings of the Academy of Political Science (Academy of Political Science) XVIII (No. 3): 269

[2] These names were found in James Slack and Nicola Boden, "Jacqui Smith's latest disaster: Banned U.S. shock jock never even tried to visit Britain - now he's suing," *Daily Mail*, May 7, 2009, http://www.dailymail.co.uk/news/ article-1177428/Jacqui-Smiths-latest-disaster-Banned-U-S-shock-jock-tried-visit-Britain--hes-suing.html (Last viewed July 23, 2009).

[3] David Harsanyi, "Fairness Doctrine Limits Free Speech," *Real Clear Politics*, June 27, 2008, http://www.realclearpolitics.com/articles/2008/06/ fairness_doctrine_limits_free.html (Last viewed on July 31, 2009).

[4] Simon Walters, "Dear Mr Editor, That Jacqui Smith is doing a fabulous job, her HUSBAND writes to newspaper," *Daily Mail* (December 21, 2008), http://www.dailymail.co.uk/news/article-1099177/Dear-Mr-Editor-That-Jacqui-Smith-doing-fabulous-job-HUSBAND-writes-newspaper.html (Last viewed July 9, 2009).

[5] Christopher Hope, "Jacqui Smith has no idea whether illegal immigrants are working at Home Office," *The Telegraph*, September 24, 2008, http:// www.telegraph.co.uk/news/3075219/Jacqui-Smith-has-no-idea-whether-illegal-immigrants-are-working-at-Home-Office.html (Last viewed on July 17, 2009).

[6] Of course, Smith's time in office was ended, exactly as I said it would be.

3

Why Michael Savage Was Targeted

When the former British Home Secretary who banned me, Jacqui Smith, was confronted about her arbitrary decision, she was unrepentant. Conservatives in Parliament told her that including me on her "name and shame" list was "ludicrous," but she would not back down. They asked Smith if "on reflection" she had come to realize that she had made a mistake. She was insistent: "No, I do not."[1] Smith insisted that I was dangerous and would incite violence against Muslims. In vain did Conservatives point out that her charges ignored the facts.

Frankly, her claims about me are merely excuses. She has publicly condemned the innocent! She obviously felt that she could not back down without admitting to a failure of judgment and a misuse of her authority. Even more important, she had to cover for the highest levels of the Labour Government, including the Prime Minister. So she had to develop a list of arguments to prove that I was properly banned from Britain for the crime of saying things she and her friends do not like.

Even now that she has stepped down in disgrace, admitted she was not competent at her job, and confessed that any successes were due to "luck," she has still not backed down from her libel of me. Now that the secret emails have been revealed, it appears that she is really still doing her job—covering for Gordon Brown. Her resignation, while a victory for me, may really simply be a ploy to pretend that she was the problem, not the Prime Minister.

Even though she has put forward a defense of her decision, as I will argue below in this chapter, the British Government kept the charges vague enough so that I really have no idea exactly what I have done wrong.

These excuses she made for picking me out for punishment for my speech should not be confused with the reasons that I have been singled out. I have been singled out because I am a not a globalist (like the Labour Party, or the Obama Administration), but a nationalist who thinks that Americans, and the citizens of every other country, have a right to maintain their borders, their language, and their culture. Neither we, nor any other nation, are obligated to ignore our own interests or those who would bring an end to our national identities.

This is what lies behind the British government's false charge that I provoke "intercommunity tensions." As globalists, they think anyone who supports nationalism is causing trouble among all the immigrant groups that are encouraged to demand their right to our cultural benefits without actually respecting our culture. My message is that the United States has the right to exist and the government is supposed to maintain its existence rather than bring about its end!

Globalism claims to support diverse communities, but it actually does nothing of the kind. It really wants all nations and cultures to become "one nation under Goldman Sachs," with profits and liberty for these bankers.

What Globalism Stands For

Globalism is often thought to simply mean international trade and peace between nations, but it really means conglomerating nations so that their identities are relegated to secondary importance. This works to the advantage (at least for awhile) of political power brokers, financiers, and some multi-national corporations. But it comes at the expense of the majority of the people in each nation.

So, for instance, the United States government seeks power by getting loans from China in order to increase government spending, even though this means this puts the nation under Chinese influence. This works to the personal advantage of a few people in power, but not to the advantage of the average citizen or of the American nation.

Or, in England, globalism means that immigration from Islamic countries is permitted even when it obviously endangers the native population. One year after the horrific attacks in England on July 7, 2005 that killed 56 people, British newspapers reported on surveys of attitudes among the Muslim immigrant population. These bombs had been planted by four Muslims, and the surveys found disturbing news. Of two million Muslims in London, seven percent endorse suicide bombing against civilians and for attacks on British military. Other surveys found that from sixteen to twenty-one percent approved of such carnage. The percentage of men between the ages of eighteen and twenty-four years old who approve of suicide bombings climbs significantly higher—and these are the people most likely to carry out such an attack.[2]

I pointed out back then that it was more likely that the grandchild of the British Prime Minister at that time, Tony Blair, would be on a prayer rug than "Mohammed the bomb maker" would be sent back to Pakistan. It never occurred to me at the time to say that it was more likely that the British government would ban a conservative Talk Radio host rather than deal with a violent subculture.

Savage: Enemy of Globalism

Globalism is a bipartisan problem.

Many will assume, when they hear that I am a "conservative" talk show host who has been banned, that I am some sort of pit-bull for the Republican Party. Nothing could be further from the truth. The GOP is just as ensnared in globalism as the Democrats.

It was when we still had a Republican President that I pointed out that, as our nation is being hollowed out by illegal aliens, we are developing a picture of the hollow men who are luring them to this country. The Republicans should be defending our jobs from those who come here illegally, but they are doing nothing of the kind. Not only are they giving your jobs away, but they are giving their own jobs away.

I once said that the US Congress should be outsourced. Now it seems the Republicans have ignored my sarcasm and taken the advice to heart. I remember being shocked to learn that the California Republican Party apparently decided that no American was qualified to be their state deputy political director. Rather, they hired a foreigner here on an H-1B visa to do the job. As if this were not bad enough, the foreigner the Republicans hired was hired by *another* foreigner who is the Chief Operations Officer of the California Republican Party. Neither of these individuals are American citizens. Neither of them understands the political landscape of the country. Neither of them can vote. But what they can do is demonstrate the suicidal attitude of Republicans who have sold out the United States of America. In this case, the self-inflicted damage was soon revealed because they actually ran afoul of immigration laws. The *San Francisco Chronicle* reported,

> California Republican Party officials might have violated federal immigration law by hiring an Australian immigrant for a top finance post without ever demanding to see his proof of legal residence, immigration officials said Tuesday.

> Ron Nehring, who heads the California Republican Party, admitted Tuesday that he–and as far as he knows, any party officials–never saw the green card that would prove that Michael Kamburowski, an Australian citizen hired as the state GOP's chief operations officer, was a legal resident.

The Republicans are so oblivious to immigration law that they actually need the U.S. government to remind them. It is "the responsibility of the employers to check and see that someone is legally in the country and eligible to work," explained a spokeswoman for the U.S. Department of Homeland Security Immigration and Customs Enforcement Division. So it seems that the GOP in California not only hired an alien, but an illegal alien.

The globalist wing of the Republican Party is not conservative. Globalists are not concerned about American sovereignty. Borders are antiquated impediments to them. The idea that America should exist as a nation is repugnant to them. There are no Americans left in the globalist wing of the Republican Party. There are only leftists, foreigners, and betrayers.

And what became of our "great" Republican President, George W. Bush, during his terms in office? He toured the nation trying to revive the Amnesty Bill. He sent his lapdogs to tell Americans that the illegals we have today in this country work harder than any other previous generation of immigrants. He told us to our faces that it is in our best economic and security interests to let illegals into the country.

Bush is now the defunct head of a defunct movement whose only purpose seems to have been to destroy our nation from within. There is nothing grand about the Grand Old Party, and GOP now seems to stand for Graying Old Prima Donnas.

America has told the globalists *no*. No illegals, no foreign influence in government, no amnesty. But the globalists have said, "Screw you. We're doing it anyway," to the American people. I have exhorted my audience to end the influence of the globalists! The next time someone in the Republican Party asks you for a donation, tell them to ask an illegal. The next time they ask you to register as a Republican, tell them you are a Nationalist. The next time they ask you for their vote, ask them this:

- *Where were you when they opened our borders?*
- *Where were you when they took away my language?*
- *Where were you when they destroyed our culture in the name of global corporatism?*

Stop them before they drown the United States of America in an irreversible flood of illegal aliens.

After the GOP lost the White House in 2008, globalism became even more dominant and nationalism became even weaker. What kind of leadership do we now have? Are the Obama Administration's policies in the best interests of the American people? On illegal immigration, their policies seem to represent the best interests not of America, but of Mexico. Obama is calling for amnesty for illegal immigrants again.

On trade, their policies represent the best interests not of the United States, but of China. We continue to depend on them to loan us money and supply us with goods we ought to be making ourselves. On terrorism, their policies represent the best interests not of the US and the West, but of the terrorists themselves. They are concerned more about the sensitivities of the mullahs than those of Main Street America.

The bottom line with the Obama Administration is that they act more like a foreign government than our government. On issue after issue, they pander to foreign powers. This administration is full of men and women without a country. They are globalists, not nationalists. So let them poll the Arab street. Let them globetrot with the Jihadists. Let them go ahead and follow their "good neighbor policy." But politics, like charity, begins at home. And unless this administration comes home, they will not remain popular.

If they do remain popular, then I suspect we will join in the fate we see unfolding in Britain and Europe right now.

European Decadence Unable to Tolerate a Critical American

When a man is trying to get away with a lie, what he can't stand is for someone to tell the truth. There is a reason why globalists need to suppress free speech. It is because they feel vulnerable to having their policies exposed. They *should* feel vulnerable!

While Britain and most of Europe expresses all sorts of international ideals–or rather, international ambitions–what we actually find is a culture that is dying and refuses to see it. Consider this description of Italy, for example:

> There are hundreds of stores in the Fiumara Mall—Sephora, Elan, Lavazza Café. But in a nation long known for its hordes of children, there is not one toy store in the sprawling mix, and a shiny merry-go-round stands dormant.
>
> "This is a place for old people," said Francesco Lotti, 24, strolling with his fiancée in Genoa's medieval old town. "Just look around. You don't see young people." Even for people their age, "there are not many places–no clubs, for example." Playgrounds? He looks quizzically at his fiancée. They can count them on a few fingers.[3]

Instead of native Italians having children, virtually the only population growth in Italy comes from immigrants. The birth rate in Genoa, for example, is actually half the death rate!

The reason for the demographic implosion is no secret. "Low birthrates in Italy began almost three decades ago, around the time women's liberation took off here."[4] Now, a quarter of native Italian women don't have children at all, and another quarter stop at one.

Italy is one of the lowest birth rates of the European nations, but it is not the only one in danger. It is estimated that twenty percent of all children in Britain have one foreign parent.[5] In order to maintain a culture, the birth rate needs to be 2.1 live births for every woman. But according to the UK's *Daily Mail*,

> In 2005, the European average was 1.38. In Ireland it was 1.9, France 1.89, Germany 1.35 and in Italy 1.23. Britain scored in the middle of this range with 1.6, but that was because–like France–we have a large Muslim population with a high birth rate. Indeed, Muslims are outbreeding non-Muslims throughout Europe.

> "Just look at the development within Europe," said a triumphant Norwegian imam a few months ago, "where the number of Muslims is expanding like mosquitoes. Every Western woman in the EU is producing an average of 1.4 children. Every Muslim woman in the same countries is producing 3.5 children. Our way of thinking will prove more powerful than yours."[6]

So what does Jacqui Smith of the Home Office do? How does she protect the English people and serve the best interests of the United Kingdom? She bans me from Britain for expressing political speech. She is so defensive that she can't even stomach one man expressing his opinion.

I suppose I should be happy to have such a pure example of the globalist ethic to show my listeners and readers. Rather than deal with the real and dire problems facing Britain, the Labour government prefers to shoot the messenger. This is no surprise. Acknowledging the factors that have created this disastrous situation would mean repudiating the factors that have been promoted by Globalists as progress and freedom. As the *Daily Mail* article points out, the decline in Ireland's birth rates has everything to do with the rise of feminism and a modern consumer society that encourage careers and discouraged children so that now: "It is a world where one child families abound and to have more than two children is to be regarded as eccentric and probably environmentally irresponsible."[7] Dealing with the issues facing England and Ireland would mean facing up to this basic wrong turn from a traditional society to one based on consumerism.

Even as the United Kingdom dies, the British government would rather practice censorship than acknowledge what they have wrought.

Anchors Away

Compared to Europe, the United States is in much better shape. But we are not lacking our own severe immigration problems. To name just one example, as I have said on *The Savage Nation*, the anchor baby situation in this nation has reached a point of crisis. The advanced guard of an invading army is slipping birth by birth across our borders each day and we are doing nothing to stop it. The anchor babies that allow more and more illegal aliens into our nation are a weight that is sinking our ship of state.

What are the risks to the health of American citizens? There is TB. There is cholera. There is leprosy. What are the financial costs? Just the price of educating these illegal alien anchor babies alone has been estimated at 5 billion dollars each and every year.

And when the cost associated with bringing the mothers and fathers and brothers and sisters and aunts and uncles and cousins of these anchor babies into the country is taken into consideration, the figure will be many times that. All this to pay for the hospitals, the schools, the welfare, and the jails that take the brunt of the illegal invasion.

And what is the risk to our sovereignty? When millions of aliens stream into our country who refuse to work, who refuse to obey our laws, who refuse to adopt our way of life, and refuse to swear loyalty to the United States of America, what happens to our nation? It evaporates; it dissipates; it slips quietly into catatonic oblivion. The nation dies to serve a globalist ideal; its borders, language, and culture disintegrate.

But I and my listeners will not let it go quietly. 360,000 anchor babies are born in the U.S. every year, and they must be stopped. The border hospitals, where 80 percent of the babies born are to illegal parents, must be forever closed to them. We must cut the dead weight that is sinking our ship of state.

The Fourteenth Amendment, as it is interpreted by the liberal courts, currently allows illegal aliens to have babies in the U.S. who automatically become citizens. We must amend the Constitution to specify that only children of citizens and legal immigrants are allowed citizenship. Stem the tide of anchor babies. Stop the flow of illegal aliens. We must change the Fourteenth Amendment to the United States Constitution.

We must save the ship of state before she sinks further into the deep waters of liberal idiocy. We must change the Fourteenth Amendment to allow only the children of citizens and legal aliens to become citizens.

Sadly, we too have leaders who, like the British government, use their power to penalize those who speak strongly on this vital issue. As we will review in Chapter Four, already government power is being used to associate those individuals who are concerned about immigration with terrorism.

How I am Being Used as a Target

I've mentioned that I am being targeted to send out a message to others. I'm targeted in part, I am sure, as a representative of Talk Radio due to my success in that medium. Also, I am targeted, as I have said, because I am a nationalist and not a globalist.

But, in a way, to make these claims is almost too charitable to the ambitious national leaders and bureaucrats in their drive for a new global economic and political order. To see what I mean, ask yourself one question: *What exactly could Michael Savage restrain himself from saying that would have entailed that he would be permitted the exquisite privilege of visiting Britain?*

There is no answer to that question.

Yes, the Home Office has published some out-of-context quotations to justify what it has done to me. But no one in the British government has ever said that, if I had not said those things, then I would be welcome in Britain. I hear that British MP David Winnick went on a TV show to agree with the decision against me because of what he believes I said about autism.[8] Aside from Winnick's total misunderstanding of my beliefs, how is my opinion on that issue, no matter now disagreeable to him or anyone else, grounds for banning me from England? They are not grounds for anything of the sort. Such reasoning was astutely mocked in a *Guardian* editorial, "Yes Jacqui, let's keep out those dangerous homeopaths."[9]

So why am I banned? What is the speech that is not permitted that can be objectively described and listed so that people know what not to say to allow them into that wonderful country of freedom and democracy and the rule of law? The answer, of course, is that no one really can know what exactly I said that got me banned. That is why the *Guardian* editorial said that "the ban on Savage is so far from being a comprehensible act, so staggeringly capricious and stupid, as to defy evaluation," and that the Home Office "might as well have defended a ban on a foreign rabbit or an offensive mango."[10]

The "rule of law" has seen better days in Merry England. The point of banning me is not to give anyone real usable information about what they may or may not say or write or believe. The point is to spread vague haunting fear about ever saying anything that a powerful politician or bureaucrat might not want to hear you say. This will mean that your only path to true safety is to positively agree with the politicians and bureaucrats. "Free speech" will mean the right to agree with the government to make sure you are not harassed or punished in some way.

While it is true that the British Home Office is sending a vague message that one must "not be like Michael Savage," it is doing so without letting people know where the actual boundaries are. So they are really sending the people a deeper message: *You must be exactly like us. You must think that we are great. You must be open-minded, tolerant, and multi-cultural like we are, or you will be cast out of our great society.*

That is a message I believe is worth resisting, not only by the British, but also by Americans. As we will see, the American government is working to produce the same fear of exercising the right of free speech.

Chapter Notes

1 Lester Haines, "Wacky Jacqui defends Michael Savage ban," *The Register* (May 19, 2009), http://www.theregister.co.uk/2009/05/19/ jacqui_smith_savage/ (Seen on July 13, 2009).

2 Daniel Pipes, "Trouble in Londonistan," *Front Page News*, July 12, 2006, http://www.frontpagemag.com/Printable.aspx?ArtId=3614 (Last viewed on July14, 2009).

3 Elisabeth Rosenthal, "Empty playgrounds in an aging Italy," *New York Times*, September 4, 2006, http://www.nytimes.com/2006/09/04/world/europe/04iht-birth2.2694069.html?_r=1&pagewanted=print (Last viewed on July 14, 2009).

4 Ibid.

5 Ibid.

6 Ruth Dudley Edwards, "Will Britain one day be Muslim?," *The Daily Mail*, May 5, 2007, http://www.dailymail.co.uk/news/article-452815/ Will-Britain-day-Muslim.html (Last viewed on July 14, 2009).

7 Ibid.

8 Boris Johnson, "Michael Savage poses no risk to British security so why won't MPs say so?" *The Telegraph*, May 10, 2009, http://www.telegraph.co.uk/comment/columnists/borisjohnson/5304788/Michael-Savage-poses-no-risk-to-British-security-so-why-wont-MPs-say-so.html (Last viewed on July 22, 2009)

9 Catherine Bennet, "Yes, Jacqui, let's keep out those dangerous homeopaths," *Guardian*, May 10, 2009, http://www.guardian.co.uk/commentisfree/2009/may/10/michael-savage-radio-homeopathy-jacqui-smith (Last viewed on August 17, 2009).

10 Ibid.

4

Big Sis Is Amiss

On each landing, opposite the lift shaft,
the poster with the enormous face gazed from the wall.
It was one of those pictures which are so contrived
that the eyes follow you about when you move.
BIG BROTHER IS WATCHING YOU,
the caption beneath it ran.

These well-known words from the first page of George Orwell's master-ful dystopian novel, *1984*, describe a central feature of slavery under a dictator-government. It is not just that you are constantly watched for any possible crime against the state (or anything that someone might think might lead to a crime against the state). Don't get me wrong, being under constant surveillance by the state is horrible. But the other aspect of Orwell's fictional world is just as controlling and even more damaging.

The citizens of such a country are constantly intimidated by their government. They are put on alert that they are being watched. This is more effective than mere surveillance since it pressures people to conform their behavior to the desires of the spies in their government since they can't be sure at any time if their behavior or attitudes might bring them unwanted attention from the authorities.

Publicly punishing a talk radio host fits easily into this picture. What the British Home Office did to me is not an anomaly. My situation may be unique for now as a radio talk show, publicly and officially lumped together with convicted killers, but all signs show that the United States government is also experimenting in this kind of action. It is undeniable that Jacqui Smith's assault on me fits in a context. There are other "Jacqui Smiths," and they are a great deal closer to us than London.

Big Sister Is Watching You!

While the slogan of George Orwell's dictatorship was "Big Brother Is Watching You," in Obama's America, Janet Napolitano is in charge of Homeland Security, so the slogan could well be changed to "Big Sister Is Watching You."

It turns out that Big Sis issued a report that warns against the possibility of violence by so-called "right-wing extremists." What did Big Sis say these violent right-wingers are concerned about? They worry about illegal aliens, the increasing power of the federal government, gun grabs, abortion and the loss of U.S. National Sovereignty. In other words, anyone who is worried about preserving our borders, language, and culture is on Big Sis' watch list.

This was not the first time this kind of government report intimating conservatives as terrorists has come up. A similar report was leaked from a "Fusion Center" in Missouri. What's a Fusion Center, you ask?

Fusion Centers: A Government Spy Network on Americans

The hot new thing among the American elite used to be fusion cuisine, combining different cooking styles from different countries. Now the hot new thing among the American elite is Fusion Centers. They're a set of local intelligence centers across the country created by the Department of Homeland Security to combat terrorism and related criminal activity.

Janet Napolitano is a zealous supporter of these new institutions. When she spoke at the National Fusion Center Conference in March 2009, she declared that they are "the centerpiece of state, local, federal intelligence-sharing for the future." She even promised, "The Department of Homeland Security will be working and aiming its programs to underlie Fusion Centers."[1]

So it came as no surprise that one of these centers produced a report that contained the same kind of "profiling" against conservatives that was also found in Napolitano's own report when it was later released. In February 2009, the

Missouri Information Analysis Center (MIAC) released a "MIAC Strategic Report" on "The Modern Militia Movement." According to the report, if you're an anti-abortion activist, if you've supported third-party presidential candidates, or if you believe that there are people in high places working to ensure that the U.S., Mexico, and Canada will someday form a North American Union, then you may be specially targeted by the Department of Homeland Security. Here is an example of the report's "intelligence":

> *Political paraphernalia:* Militia members most commonly associated with 3rd party political groups. It is not uncommon for militia members to display Constitutional Party, Campaign for Liberty, or Libertarian material. These members are usually supporters of former Presidential Candidates: Ron Paul, Chuck Baldwin, and Bob Barr.

So, according to this report, if you display a bumper sticker supporting a third-party candidate, or if you possess a DVD of a documentary against the income tax, you could well be a member of a domestic paramilitary group. The iron heel is obviously starting to come down.

Lest we get carried away against the Democratic Party and the Obama Presidency, let's remember that the Homeland Security Department and these Fusion Centers were not created by Obama, but were created by George W. Bush. And while Obama may ultimately be responsible for suppressing third parties and anyone else whose thinking is out of line with the Marxist mainstream, it was Bush who started the process. So do yourself a favor and ignore lockstep Republicans who insist that this is all Obama's doing. Both sides are to blame. Bush started it, and Obama may finish it.

In the uproar that followed the leaking of the MIAC Strategic Report, there seemed to be a backing down on the part of the Government's spymasters and intimidators. After all, Missouri's Democratic governor, Jay Nixon, eventually "distanced his administration from the process that allowed the release of a report linking support for libertarian and conservative causes to domestic terrorism."[2] Surely that means conservatives won, right?

No! At least, not yet.

It is quite clear that the Fusion Center bureaucracy is not going to do or say anything that would detract from their sense of their own importance. On June 10, at hearings concerning the report, Col. James Keathley of the Missouri Highway Patrol would not even admit that the writer of the report had been "overzealous." His reply to such a description? "I don't know,"[3] Actually, I agree. To describe the report writing as "overzealous" implies that it was a good idea but that the writing accidentally went "too far."

Not at all! The report was an act of intimidation and a banana republic manifesto from the beginning. But I'm afraid that's not what Keathley meant. He meant that the content of the report was arguably sober and appropriate.

He also gave this less-than-assuring account of how the government tracks the difference between criminals and those who disagree with the government:

> One key question from lawmakers: How does law enforcement differentiate between a passionate political protester and a deranged and potentially dangerous threat? Keathley said that's a difficult question to answer, and characterized it as "a thin line." "Obviously, I think we're all struggling with this Fusion Center concept and this intelligence concept is fairly new. It is difficult to make those decisions," Keathley said.[4]

Yes, it is fairly new, because it is completely un-American to have the government spying on people for their political beliefs! We are indeed struggling because the whole concept is completely unconstitutional. A thin line indeed!

A Sheriff actually defended the Fusion Center by saying, "To think that we would not do strategic work within the fusion center is to say that it's okay to commit certain acts of violence." What nonsense! Acts of violence have been illegal and considered reprehensible throughout the history of the United States long before the Bush Administration decided to establish an elaborate spying network to pry into the lives of the American people.

While people who are supposed to enforce American law can't see what is wrong about this report, even the ACLU has responded to this by saying that it crosses the line and shows a disregard for civil liberties. One of their reports looks at a Fusion Center in LA which instructs the LAPD to report and pass on to intelligence agencies anyone displaying one or more of sixty-five behaviors, even if they are "non-criminal." These behaviors can include "such innocuous, clearly subjective, and First Amendment-protected activities as: taking measurements, using binoculars, taking pictures or video footage 'with no apparent esthetic value,' abandoning vehicle, drawing diagrams, taking notes, and espousing extremist views."5

So, the Constitution says that one has freedom to espouse views that people in government might find extreme, and the Fusion Centers want to put you on a government list when you do so. Remember, if you go out and decide to bird watch with binoculars or spend time outdoors writing in your journal, Big Sis is watching you.

With the ACLU's sane public stance, dissidents on the left and dissidents on the right agree for once. But the government media complex, the Bush-Obama crowd, seems to be just fine with the idea of sending you up the river if you support a third party, or putting you under surveillance if you have subversive literature, or if you happen to support the wrong Republican member of Congress.

The DHS Report

Even though Fusion Centers are part of the Department of Homeland Security, the MIAC strategic report was regarded by many people as mostly a local Missouri problem. Any hope that the trouble was isolated to one small group or state came to an end when an Assessment Report by the Department of Homeland Security was officially released, *Rightwing Extremism: Current Economic and Political Climate Fueling Resurgence in Radicalization and Recruitment.*

Unlike the MIAC report leaked by a concerned police officer, this report was purposefully revealed to the nation. It clearly used the excuse of national security to marginalize and set the stage for criminalizing political dissent. So, for example, it included in its definition of dangerous "Rightwing extremism…"

> …those that are mainly antigovernment, rejecting federal authority
> in favor of state or local authority, or rejecting government author-
> ity entirely. It may include groups and individuals that are dedicat-
> ed to a single issue, such as opposition to abortion or immigration.

The report goes on this way, casting suspicion on anyone who holds conservative positions on a variety of issues, letting the public know that it is leading law enforcement officers to spy on them and treat them with suspicion. If you care about illegal immigration or the Second Amendment you will be targeted by Homeland Security "partnering" with local law enforcement.

The Report makes a big deal about the "parallel" situation in the 1990s to today. In doing so, it makes claims about the situation leading up to the Oklahoma City Bombing in 1995:

> The current economic and political climate has some similarities to the 1990s when right-wing extremism experienced a resurgence fueled largely by an economic recession, criticism about the outsourcing of jobs, and the perceived threat to U.S. power and sovereignty by other foreign powers.

Recession? The economy in 1995 is something most people would love to return to. It was a prosperous growing economy, even if Bill Clinton had talked it down during his earlier campaign (there was brief economic discomfort in the beginning of the decade, but that was short-lived).

The real parallel between the two situations is that in both cases we have a Leftist Democratic President. That is obviously the one and only reason to invoke the history of the 1990s, but the writers of the report were too dishonest to admit what they were doing. So instead they wrote about a recession that never happened. In fact, the only thing the report mentions about the President is that he is African-American, not that he is a neo-Marxist. The people at Homeland Security cannot even admit to themselves that the tension is caused by political ideology. They self-servingly insist that it is racism. These are pretty standard tactics in the media—ignore the substance of the issues and assert that all your opponents are racists. But it is much, much worse for people with the power to use weapons and prisons to engage in this sort of convenient fantasy. The report claims that there are dangers from private citizens, but invoking the 1990s more clearly shows us that it is the government that is the real threat in this case.

> Proposed imposition of firearms restrictions and weapons bans likely would attract new members into the ranks of right-wing extremist

groups, as well as potentially spur some of them to begin planning and training for violence against the government. The high volume of purchases and stockpiling of weapons and ammunition by right-wing extremists in anticipation of restrictions and bans in some parts of the country continue to be a primary concern to law enforcement.

Stockpiling weapons a concern to law enforcement? With the appeal to the 1990s it is hard not to think of the botched Waco raid, the questionable violence that looked like it was due to a desire to appear tough on television. In fact, the report itself admits this:

> During the 1990s, rightwing extremist hostility toward government was fueled by the implementation of restrictive gun laws... and the federal law enforcement's handling of the confrontations at Waco, Texas and Ruby Ridge, Idaho.

Yes, and that happened under the authority of another Big Sister, Janet Reno, the head of the FBI. After the women and children got baked in Waco, she ran around saying, "I accept full responsibility," which is apparently code for the phrase, *I am never accountable for anything that happens on my watch, no matter how horrible and avoidable.* Nothing happened to her after her gross failure that resulted in children burned to death. If anything, the 1990s tell us that what is really threatening is when the government becomes paranoid about American citizens who stockpile weapons. Their "concern" leads to botched operations and unnecessary deaths. Liberals only worry about "collateral damage" when they are not in power.

But the most evil part of the report is the way it singles out our military. While it is bad enough that people holding conservative or constitutionalist political convictions are targeted and profiled by our government, it is much worse that they cast suspicion on the men and women of our Armed Forces who have risked their lives to defend us. The Department of Homeland Security clearly believes that our military are a real threat to peace and order.

> *Disgruntled Military Veterans:* DHS/I&A assesses that right-wing extremists will attempt to recruit and radicalize returning veterans

in order to exploit their skills and knowledge derived from military training and combat. These skills and knowledge have the potential to boost the capabilities of extremists–including lone wolves or small terrorist cells–to carry out violence. The willingness of a small percentage of military personnel to join extremist groups during the 1990s because they were disgruntled, disillusioned, or suffering from the psychological effects of war, is being replicated today.

One justification given for singling out the military is that some tiny percentage in the past has joined with white supremacist groups. It is equally true that a small percentage of the general population has joined such groups. So why not write about the need to watch everyone? Another justification is the assessment of "a prominent civil rights organization." But this turns out to be the Southern Poverty Law Center, a radical leftist group that is as hateful and paranoid as any organization can be.

On April 17, Napolitano appeared on Fox News and said, "To the extent veterans read it as an accusation…an apology is owed."[6] But that hardly matters. The problem is not just that it is an accusation. The problem is that it is a declaration of intent to spy and monitor people for nothing more than simply being soldiers, or for their political beliefs.

The DHS report is a horrible assault on our military. They should be given thanks, not issued warnings about their political opinions–which is exactly what the report does. By releasing the report, Janet Napolitano has violated the First and Fifth Amendments by attempting to chill the rights of free speech, expressive association, and equal protection. There is no way that the Constitution permits a government agency to encourage law enforcement to target and report citizens to federal officials as extremists and potential terrorists based on their political beliefs. This report needs to be legally neutralized.

If you think this report will do no harm, think again. Remember the TEA (Taxed Enough Already) Party rallies on April 15? The government has started treating these peaceful assemblies as a potential security threat. On April 9, the Maryland National Guard issued a report entitled "Planned TEA Party Protests (FPCON Advisory 09-004)," and was labeled "for official use only." It described these protests as if they were a terrorist risk or threat. For example:

Commanders at all levels should establish relationship with local police in order to understand the local threats. Keep family members informed. Talk to other service personnel to share information. Practice OPSEC. Don't provide personal information to anyone you don't know. Avoid high risk areas.

Commanders are encouraged to update alert rosters and review emergency evacuation plans/rally points. Ensure all facilities have emergency phone lists posted (i.e. FBI, FIRE, POLICE, HOSPITALS, EMS, ETC...). Be aware of and avoid local protests. Report all potential protest activities to your next higher headquarters.

This report appeared two days after the DHS report was published. You may have seen these "local threats" on television. Other than harassment from news reporters, it is hard to understand what sort of high risk was present at these peaceful protests. The government is obviously doing all it can to encourage dangerous paranoia among the National Guard and police. This, in turn, is designed to intimidate conservatives into hiding what they believe.

Eventually, conservative outrage forced Napolitano to withdraw the report. My listeners made their voices heard. While this is a real victory, it doesn't change the fact that we have been put on notice of what our government thinks of us.

Debbie Stabenow: A Big Sister Who Advocates Censorship For the Sake of Corruption

Obviously, Liberalism is on the offensive. The MIAC report and the DHS report both fit well with the calls for the re-establishment of the Fairness Doctrine. Leftists are coming out of the woodwork to attack conservative Talk Radio. While Obama keeps claiming to have no agenda to do so, he has taken unprecedented action in singling out a talk radio personality. He publicly told Republican congressmen that you can't get things done by listening to talk radio.

Another "Big Sis" wannabe, Senator Debbie Stabenow of Michigan, provides us with insight into what happens when lawmakers grab at unconstitutional power. Not only does this Sister want to re-establish the Fairness Doctrine, but she has declared that she wanted hearings on radio accountability.

Here is the exchange she had with a liberal talk radio host:

> **Liberal Mouthpiece:** Yeah, I mean look: They have a right to say that. They've got a right to express that. But, they should not be the only voices heard. So, is it time to bring back the Fairness Doctrine?
>
> **Senator Debbie Stabenow (D-MI):** I think it's absolutely time to pass a standard. Now, whether it's called the Fairness Standard, whether it's called something else—I absolutely think it's time to be bringing accountability to the airwaves. I mean, our new president has talked rightly about accountability and transparency. You know, that we all have to step up and be responsible. And, I think in this case, there needs to be some accountability and standards put in place.
>
> **Liberal Mouthpiece:** Can we count on you to push for some hearings in the United States Senate this year, to bring these owners in and hold them accountable?
>
> **Senator Debbie Stabenow (D-MI):** I have already had some discussions with colleagues and, you know, I feel like that's gonna happen. Yep.[7]

Nothing like show trials to empower the current regime!

It has become almost a cliché to accuse me of hate speech. I firmly believe that the voices calling for the suppression of free speech are the ones that should be recognized as voices of hate. But "hate" may be too pure a word to use to describe Big Sis Stabenow's motivation for wanting show trials about the Fairness Doctrine. Greed is also playing a part. Stabenow's husband, Thomas Athans, co-founded the liberal TalkUSA Radio network. He is now the Executive Vice-President of liberal *Air America*.

This is all about corruption! How can liberal talk radio survive in the market? *It can't and it doesn't.*

So Liberals want to make sure that liberal shows don't have to deal with a free market. They want the Fairness Doctrine to empower the FCC to force stations to broadcast their shows as "equal time." Stabenow is actually after a government bailout for another ailing industry, Left Wing Talk Radio. I'm not sure how they could argue that Liberal talk radio is "too big to fail," since it has always been a tiny industry.

This is a perfect example of one reason you don't want to give a government agency too much unaccountable power. The people who make the decisions will do so for private reasons rather than the public good. The Fairness Doctrine is a way to increase the personal profits of Stabenow's husband's business.

How will "fairness" do this? The "Fairness Doctrine" kills entertaining conservative talk radio with boredom. It means that, when anyone complains, the radio station owners are compelled to match every single moment of conservative opinion with liberal opinion. Suddenly radio becomes as boring as National Public Radio. Who would listen to these hours of liberal pontificating? Not many people. Who is going to want to advertise and sponsor these hours? No one!

The Fairness Doctrine makes talk radio economically impossible. It straddles radio stations with dead air that produces no income. It ends conservative talk radio, and leaves the United States with nothing but NPR and the mainstream liberal media. These networks always claim to be doing "neutral journalism" so that the Fairness Doctrine is never fairly applied to them! Everyone knows that conservative talk radio did not exist until the FCC stopped the Fairness Doctrine. Stabenow wants to go back to that time for reasons that are both political and profitable to her family's fortunes.

It is not by any means the only example. Al Gore has openly called for police-state censorship on behalf of what is treated as the Biggest Sister of all: Mother Nature. He wants Attorney Generals to punish any company that advocates clean coal as an investment that will help the alleged "global warming" crisis. He mentioned this in a speech advocating civil disobedience to stop clean coal technology from being used. His specific excuse was that it is lawful to practice this kind of censorship because it constitutes "fraud."

> "I believe for a carbon company to spend money convincing the stock-buying public that the risk from the global climate crisis is not that great represents a form of stock fraud because they are misrepresenting a material fact," he said. "I hope these state attorney generals around the country will take some action on that."[8]

It almost seems like, for liberals, "free speech" really means nothing more than "easy, legal, widespread, and mainstream access to porn." When it comes to any kind of political speech they don't like, advocacy of censorship rolls off their lips without even hesitancy or a mild stutter that would show that they recognize they are doing anything un-American.

It reminds me of the campaign of intimidation waged by pro-Obama thugs in local governments. St. Louis' local KMOV news reported during the campaign on September 28, 2008, "Prosecutors and sheriffs from across Missouri are joining something called the Barak Obama Truth Squad. Two high profile prosecutors are part of the team."[9]

The purpose of this goon squad was to threaten to prosecute anyone who claimed that Obama would raise taxes on anyone making less than $250,000 per year, or who denied that Obama was a Christian.

But, just as in the case of Stabenow, once again the advocacy of the power to censor is motivated by greed.

> Deepening his ties to Silicon Valley, former Vice President Al Gore said on Monday that he had become a partner in the venture capital firm Kleiner Perkins Caufield & Byers.
>
> The alliance provides Mr. Gore an additional pulpit for his advocacy of environmental causes, but also gives the Nobel laureate an opportunity to nurture green businesses.
>
> Venture capitalists said the move could help companies financed by Kleiner establish ties with big business and government, and obtain subsidies that encourage broader use of new technologies.
>
> Mr. Gore's part-time duties will entail investigating the growth potential of start-up companies focused on the alternative energy sector, and then weighing in on whether Kleiner Perkins should finance those companies.
>
> Mr. Gore said he would donate his salary from the venture to the Alliance for Climate Protection, a nonprofit policy foundation.[10]

This is basically a PR press release being used as a story. This is a massive conflict of interest, and what Gore says about the Alliance for Climate Protection simply tells us that Gore is escaping taxation. You almost have to admire his sheer brazen shamelessness.

When confronted about his obvious conflict of interest by Representative Marsha Blackburn (R-Tenn)–in an extremely polite and deferential manner–Gore sneeringly and self-righteously blasted her with the fact that a non-profit under his control, and that he directly benefits from, was getting all the untaxable money.[11] *No, I don't just profit from my partnership in a venture capital firm, I profit from it without paying a dime of it to the IRS.*

Well, how can anyone question that great stand for integrity?

What Gore has is an expanding pile of tax-exempt money to fund his personal aides and from which to get honorariums and many other perks. None of this is revealed or investigated in the *New York Times* piece. The closest they get is quoting someone who points out that it is Gore's political connections rather than his business savvy that led them to make Gore a partner: Anyone who thinks this is happening because Al has fantastic clean-tech entrepreneurial chops is fooling themselves. Rather, green energy "is a policy issue, a political issue, and that requires connections to get things done."[12] True, but it hardly even scratches the surface of what this means. Many people have a great economic interest in making sure alternative energy is pursued. And it even reaches the point where Al Gore publicly advocates censorship on their behalf. "Kleiner Perkins declined to say whether Mr. Gore would receive a management fee or participate in profit sharing, noting that matters of compensation are private."[13]

The Fairness Doctrine v. the Broadcaster Freedom Act

A generation ago Liberals said, *I may disagree with you, but I'll fight to the death for your right to say it.* I doubt they ever meant it, but at least they said it. Today liberals say, *I disagree with you, and I'll fight to the death until your right to say it is taken away.* The liberals are coming closer and closer to dismantling the First Amendment entirely. The fairness doctors who wish to impose the Fairness Doctrine are about to perform a surgery on our constitution from which the body politic may never recover.

And furthermore, the American people themselves are completely opposed to it. Poll after poll has demonstrated that the American people, even though they were tricked into voting for Chairman Obama, are still in favor of freedom of speech. We haven't fallen *that* far into communism yet.

But the Fairness Doctors have other plans for us. They're all for freedom of speech, just as long as it praises Obama to one degree or another. They're all for freedom of expression, as long as no doubts are expressed about the stimulus package, or socialist medicine, or whatever else they plan to do to us. They want you to be able to say whatever you want, but only as long as you're supporting neo-Marxism.

The only problem is, democracy doesn't work without naysayers. Democracy doesn't work without dissent. And I, Michael Savage, Dr Dissent, refuse to back down. The Republicans may have rolled over. Senators Arlen Specter, Susan Collins and Olympia Snowe may have gone along to survive.[14] The editors of the *Meekly Standard* may be dining with Obama, but I won't. We must stop the Fairness Doctors before they kill our country.

The Savage Nation has repeatedly exposed Liberals for what they are. California Attorney General and former governor Jerry Brown was a guest on *The Savage Nation* recently. When I asked him about re-imposing the Fairness Doctrine, an act I pointed out would destroy conservative talk radio, he replied that a little state control wouldn't hurt anybody.

Though he later claimed that the remark was intended as ironic, these are the words of an elected state official. Whether intended as ironic or not, to advocate state control of the media is no small thing. A little state control *has* hurt people. It's destroyed the people of Venezuela, and it's condemned the people of Cuba to a life of misery and despotism. A little state control in North Korea and Iran may pose the world's largest security threat. And during the Twentieth Century, a little state control in Russia, Germany, China and Cambodia has caused the deaths of millions. So though Mr. Brown may have meant it ironically, when he says that a little state control has never hurt anybody, he is walking on dangerous ground.

Unfortunately, his irony seems to be taken as gospel by Senator Tom Harkin, by Senator Debbie Stabenow, and even by former President Bill Clinton, who have all advocated a little state control in the form of the Fairness Doctrine.

Recently, President Obama's top advisor, the Chicago politician David Axelrod, has refused to rule out imposing the Fairness Doctrine.

So don't listen to their excuses. Don't believe them when they say it's just an attempt to balance the medium. Ninety percent of the media is in the hands of the liberals already. Liberals are trying to stamp out the last refuge for independent news and thought: conservative talk radio and *The Savage Nation*.

However, I should mention that one of the last honest men in the United States Senate, South Carolina Senator Jim DeMint, has stood up and fired back against all the neo-Marxist censors who would like to destroy the freedom of speech by imposing the fairness doctrine on America. He is a sponsor of the Broadcaster Freedom ACT which would prevent the FCC from re-imposing the Fairness Doctrine. This bill

> Amends the Communications Act of 1934 to prohibit the Federal Communications Commission (FCC), notwithstanding any other provision of any Act, from having the authority to require broadcasters to present opposing viewpoints on controversial issues of public importance, commonly referred to as the Fairness Doctrine.[15]

In response I say, *Bravo, Senator!* Somebody in power is standing up!

Though Obama is busy pretending that he doesn't want the Fairness Doctrine, he's lined up all his attack dogs to push for it. Nancy Pelosi, Dick Durbin, Debbie Stabenow, Chuck Schumer, Tom Harkin and Diane Feinstein have all declared that they want the Fairness Doctrine. But DeMint challenged the US Senate and the entire country to answer the question: *Do you support free speech or do you want to silence voices you disagree with?*

Because, you see, when this country was created, the founders declared that, "Congress shall make no law... abridging the freedom of speech, or of the press." Now some in Congress would like to change those words to abridge freedom of speech for those whose opinions make them *uncomfortable*. But a few brave men and women in the Senate said that is unacceptable. The Broadcaster Freedom Act had 31 co-sponsors, including Kit Bond of Missouri, Sam Brownback of Kansas, Jim Bunning of Kentucky, Tom Coburn of Oklahoma, John Cornyn of Texas,

Lindsey Graham of South Carolina, Kay Bailey-Hutchison of Texas, James Inhofe of Oklahoma, Mitch McConnell of Kentucky and Jeff Sessions of Alabama.

Sadly, though not that unexpectedly, the Democrat majority would not pass this bill. In fact, they used their powers to prevent a vote so that none of them could be recorded as voting against it.[16] So at least they acknowledged that America doesn't approve of censorship. Furthermore, the Senate attached it to another bill. While this doesn't mean it will pass, it does show that there are enough Democrats in the Senate who don't want to be thought sympathetic to the legislation.[17]

Eventually, voters will see what is going on and there will be enough votes to pass it. In fact, it is no doubt public opposition that has kept Congress from being able to pass a Fairness Doctrine as yet.

The Savage Nation is not alone. The ranks of real conservatives, real liberals, and all who value the right to speak freely are rallying around this common cause.

We will not be silenced.

But we have to be ever vigilant. Even if the Fairness Doctrine never passes, there are other threats. The FCC's new "Chief Diversity Officer," Mark Lloyd, has advocated forcing private broadcasting companies to pay licensing fees equal to their total operating costs that go to directly pay for public broadcasting outlets to spend the same amount.[18] So basically, this would start a State-run radio industry to spew official propaganda that would be paid for by conservative talk radio!

Trans-Atlantic Collusion?

So there are many "big sisters" out there wanting to wash out our mouth with soap—as well as "big brothers."

- In England, Jacqui Smith who was in office long enough to ban me from Britain and label me as a companion to murderers and convicts. The British government has not backed down from Jacqui Smith's actions, even though she is no longer in office.

- In the Justice Department we have Janet Napolitano, both issuing her own report, as well as supporting Fusion Centers making reports, claiming that those involved in conservative causes are terrorist threats.

- In the Senate, we have Debbie Stabenow promoting show trials about talk radio, advocating the Fairness Doctrine, as well as working to protect her husband's interest in the business of Left wing talk radio.

- Though I haven't mentioned it yet, we also have Hillary Rodham-Clinton in the State Department.

Why would I bring Hillary's name into it? What we have is a war on free speech, political speech, and talk radio–taking place both in Britain and in the United States. I have to ask: *Are we supposed to believe that Smith's "name and shame" list and the pattern we are seeing in the United States is a coincidence?*

Let me ask more specific questions. Are we supposed to believe that the Home Office somehow discovered my show on her own? How is that possible? *The Savage Nation* doesn't even air in Britain. So who brought the show to her attention? Did some private citizen decide to contact the Secretary of the Home Office? Who would do something like that? Would they be acting purely as private citizens or also as advocates for public officials in the US?

Did someone in government decide that this would be a good way to test out a new way of censoring the Administration's enemies? I don't see how that possibility can be ruled out. It makes about as much sense as the idea of the British government finding out about me without American help. In fact, I think that *Media Matters*, a Stalinist, anti-conservative hate tank, funded by George Soros and planned by Hillary Rodham-Clinton, took some of my radio shows and edited them to create a monster-like picture of me. They then sent them to a stooge in London.

To put it another way, is it likely that the British Secretary of the Home Office would take such a drastic step without informing *anyone* in the State Department? Was no one given advance warning or asked their opinion in Hillary Clinton's bureaucracy?

Right now, the Home Office's last word on the matter is to continue to deny that there was any communication:

Nigel Evans, a leading Conservative member of parliament in Britain, addressed a question to the Secretary of State for the Home Department, asking "what discussions his department has had with the U.S. administration on the creation of the list of foreign nationals barred from entry to the U.K., with particular reference to the inclusion of Michael Savage on that list."

A reply came from Phil Woolas, Minister of State in the Home Office and a member of the Labour Party: "The Home Office did not consult the U.S. administration about the creation of the list of foreign nationals who are excluded from the United Kingdom on unacceptable behavior grounds, which included U.S. citizen, Michael Savage.

"However, following publication of the list, Home Office and FCO (Foreign and Commonwealth Office) officials have discussed the Government's policy on exclusion with American officials."[19]

So, *at the very least,* discussions started after I was banned from Britain. That much has been admitted. But I've not heard any indication that the United States government is doing anything at all to end the ban on my visiting Britain. What did US bureaucrats say to the Home Office? Did they applaud the British government's action against me? Did they encourage it? At this point it is impossible to say with certainty.

But this I can say: as far as I know, the only politicians who acted like civilized human beings were the British Tories in Parliament who strongly objected to the Labour government's war on me. In fact, when looking on both sides of the Atlantic, the list of those who have supported me and those who have not may surprise you.

Chapter Notes

[1] Testimony of Acting Under Secretary Bart R. Johnson, Office of Intelligence and Analysis, before the House Committee on Homeland Security, Subcommittee on Intelligence, Information Sharing, and Terrorism Risk Assessment, "FY2010 Budget Request," June 24, 2009, http://www.dhs.gov/ynews/testimony/testimony _1245862945214.shtm (Last viewed July 16, 2009).

[2] "Nixon distances administration from production of MIAC report; supports changes announced yesterday" Prime Buzz, *Kansas City Star*, March 26, 2009. http://primebuzz.kcstar.com/?q=node/17833 (Last viewed on July 16, 2009).

[3] David Catanese, "MIAC isn't making 'strategic' reports but won't rule them out," KY3.com, June 10, 2009, http://www.ky3.com/news/political/blog/47729602.html (Last viewed on July 16, 2009).

[4] Ibid.

[5] Mike German and Jay Stanley, "Fusion Center Update," ACLU, July 2008. http://www.aclu.org/pdfs/privacy/fusion_update_20080729.pdf (Last viewed on July 16, 2009).

[6] Bob Unroh, "Savage sues Napolitano for targeting vets," *WorldNetDaily*, April 17, 2009, http://www.wnd.com/index.php?fa=PAGE.view&pageId= 95244 (Last viewed July 18, 2009).

[7] Seton Motley, "Politico: Sen. Stabenow Wants Hearings On Radio 'Accountability'; Talks Fairness Doctrine," *NewsBusters*, February 5, 2009, http://newsbusters.org/blogs/seton-motley/2009/02/05/politico-sen-stabenow-wants-hearings-radio-accountability-talks-fairne (Last viewed on July 18, 2009).

[8] "Gore urges civil disobedience," *Reuters*, September 24, 2008.

[9] Video available online at http://www.kmov.com/video/index.html?nvid=285793&shu=1 and at http://www.youtube.com/watch?v=iStZAbf47FA

[10] Matt Ritchell, "Investment Firm Names Gore as a Partner," *New York Times*, Nov. 13, 2007. http://www.nytimes.com/2007/11/13/technology/13gore.html (Last viewed on July 20, 2009).

[11] This C-SPAN footage is on YouTube. One clip of it can be found at http:// www.youtube.com/watch?v=4eS16Pn_bHE (Last viewed on July 22, 2009).

[12] Matt Ritchell, Ibid.

[13] Ibid.

[14] The three GOP turncoats who voted for Obama's disastrous "stimulus." See Carl Hulse and David M. Herszenhorn, "Senators Reach Deal on Stimulus Plan as Jobs Vanish," *New York Times*, February 6, 2009, http://www.nytimes.com/2009/02/07/us/politics/07stimulus.html?r=2&partner=rss&emc=rss&page-wanted =all (Last viewed on July 22, 2009). Obama thanked them for their "patriotism."

[15] http://www.opencongress.org/bill/111-s34/show (Viewed July 18, 2009).

[16] Rep. Greg Walden and Rep. Mike Pence, "Dems Again Block Broadcaster Freedom Act," *Human Events*, July 22, 2009, http://www.human-events.com/article.php?id=32805 (Last viewed on July 22, 2009).

[17] "Senate Backs Amendment to Prevent 'Fairness Doctrine' Revival," Fox News, February 26, 2009, http://www.foxnews.com/politics/2009/02/26/demint-tries-prevent-fairness-doctrine-revival/ (Viewed on August 19, 2009).

[18] Matt Cover, "FCC's Chief Diversity Officer Wants Private Broadcasters to Pay a Sum Equal to Their Total Operating Costs to Fund Public Broadcasting," CNS News, August 13, 2009, http://www.cnsnews.com/news/article/52435 (Last viewed on August 19, 2009).

[19] Jim Meyers, "British Government: We Didn't Consult U.S. on Michael Savage Exclusion," *NewsMax.com*, July 1, 2009, http://www.newsmax.com/insidecover/UK_no_savage_talks/2009/07/01/231102.html

5

America and the World
React to the Attack on Savage

My personal "battle of Britain" has entailed many, many days of hell and anxiety. There has been some progress, as I will describe in detail elsewhere. But there have been many frustrations as I have failed to get the leaders in charge of Britain's government to come to their senses and act like civilized human beings.

The key thing I have to remember is the wisdom of Churchill: *Never give up. Never, never, never give up.*

However, no matter how much you feel like you are all by yourself, virtually no one can make it totally alone. I suspect that many in government or politics are aware of this basic human condition and so, when dealing with targets, do all they can to make them feel isolated. The very name of the "Name and Shame" list demonstrates this desire to alienate me in public.

So another important point to remember is that all of us should appreciate our friends and sometimes even our enemies when we are standing up for the truth. In my case, I've found help in both friends and enemies, but have also found that some (so-called) "friends," don't care all that much about free speech if I am involved.

One of the oddest discoveries is that the "conservatives" in politics in my own country have done virtually nothing to help me and defend our rights to free speech. I did get support from politicians, but it was all from British conservative politicians who could not stand how the Home Office was dragging their country down. The Shadow Secretary of the Home Office, Chris Grayling, told Jacqui Smith, "What we need from the Government is not the gimmick of a name and shame list but a consistent strategy on who can and can't come into the country."[1] If you remember what kind of aliens who are permitted to stay in Britain, as I listed in chapter two, you know he was right.

Michael Fabricant, Conservative MP for Lichfield, refused to accept Jacqui Smith's groundless allegation that I encouraged violence, saying, "the things of which she accuses Mike Savage are also illegal in the United States of America, and he has not faced prosecution there."[2] He asked rhetorically, "Does she realize how ludicrous her ban is and the disrepute into which she has put this country in the eyes of many right-seeing–and, indeed, left-seeing–people in the United States?"[3] Another Conservative MP, Crispin Blunt, said that the Home Offices ban list had provoked "completely avoidable legal action" and was "a self-evident gimmick and demeaning to Government."[4]

I Get By With a Little Help from My Enemies: The Real Liberals Support Savage

On the Internet, an unknown liberal blogger paid the Michael Savage show a compliment. He quoted *The Savage Nation* on Iraq when I said, "If we're there, let's win, or let's get the hell out of there." Then he responded, "This, unlike anything else I'd ever heard him say, made sense in what he would consider to be my mentally diseased brain."

Liberals listen to *The Savage Nation* not always because they agree with Michael Savage, but because they know that they will get honest, frank, passionate opinions here. Water will not be carried. Rings will not be kissed. Conservatives listen to *The Savage Nation* because they know I'm right. Liberals listen to *The Savage Nation* because they sense I'm right.

The story of how I have struggled against the banning of the British Government would not be complete if I didn't acknowledge the help I received, even if not personally intended, from genuine liberals who lived up to their name. I've often complained that "liberals" today are not genuine. They claim to support free speech and tolerance, but in fact advocate censorship and intolerance. While I don't want to deny or diminish my opposition to liberalism, I also don't want to ignore the people who stood up and did the right thing by me, even though they cannot possibly appreciate what I say.

I think perhaps the most amazing thing about this story of being banned in Britain is that The Council of American-Islamic Relations (CAIR), the ACLU and I *all agreed* on a legal principle. CAIR has opposed my show and called for a boycott. But they also opposed political censorship of me or my show. The spokesman, Ibrahim Hooper, told reporters, "as a matter of principle, we don't support such bans. They tend to be selective, in that only popular speech is allowed and unpopular speech is not allowed."5

A lawyer for the American Civil Liberties Union espoused the same principle, and didn't allow anyone to think that being banned from a country was anything less than censorship. He said that my banning illustrated that countries were using "their borders as a weapon of censorship." He added, "While some of these people may express views that others find disagreeable, often the cure is worse than the disease."6

There are also British liberals who have defended me, or at least attacked the Home Office for their tyrannical and libelous ruling on me.

One example would be Evgeny Morozov, a fellow at the Open Society Institute who serves on the board of OSI's Information Program. He is originally from Belarus (something I wouldn't mention, and don't really care about, in case you're wondering–except that he includes it in his blurb, so I assume he wants people to know).

Morozov wrote an editorial on May 10, 2009 that said, "I usually feel bad for people who face travel problems," and made it clear that he included me among those he sympathized with, even though he declares he does not at all like what I say or write or stand for. Nevertheless, he pointed out how incoherent it is to politically oppress people because you don't like or agree with them. "I do find it strange when a diverse and multicultural society is based on exclusion of people espousing radical views."7

He also points out that the idea that a travel ban actually can protect a nation from unwelcome ideas is simply false. He writes,

> So, let me offer one free piece of advice to all other governments: never let people who are ignorant of the inner working of the global public sphere, mediated by the Internet and 24-hour news cycle, make such sensitive decisions. Travel bans may have worked in the

pre-Internet age: after all, getting national exposure without touring the nation's universities and visiting the editorial offices of its leading newspapers may have been impossible, particularly in the class-obsessed Britain....

But this world of the past no longer exists. That is because the Internet has changed everything.

In the age of cheap and widely accessible self-publishing, all one needs is to catch a viral tide on Twitter, YouTube or Facebook and ride it as long as possible. A decision to ban Savage from entering the UK triggered more than a viral tide—it triggered a viral tsunami, which the man, if he is smart—would be riding for the next few months, making sure to appear on every semi-important news outlet in the US, UK (have they heard of satellites?), and elsewhere.

Obviously, I wish Morozov would agree with me more than he does. But I really appreciate his principled stand against using borders for censorship and his defense of free speech. I'm also glad to read his common-sense criticism of travel bans in the age of the Internet. However, I wonder if he is missing the point as to why the ban was enacted. It seems to me that, if the Home Office was truly afraid that my ideas might upset their multicultural society, they would not have drawn attention to me. A more reasonable explanation, I think, is that the Labour government wasn't really worried about the damage I could do to British multicultural society (where now more people have heard about me than ever before, thanks to her, as Morozov points out). Instead, they saw me as an opportunity to publicly teach others not to criticize the status quo nor articulate what they consider to be "extreme views."

In other words, these politicians know full-well I am not capable (nor do I want to) cause "inter-community violence." But by enacting their own political violence against me, they get to reinforce the (alleged) superiority of their own views. They get to communicate to the world that, even though censorship is normally forbidden, censorship is okay in my case.

For the record, however, I don't think *anything* about this ban is a good thing. The attention I have received, along with the increased number of listeners, are no match for the horror of being publicly singled out and persecuted in this way. This really should be a no-brainer. No private citizen feels anything but dread at being targeted by a major Western nation, especially with the total apathy (at the very least!) of one's own government.

Another insightful comment ran in the London *Telegraph* on May 10 of 2009.[8] I'm not sure if the writer, Boris Johnson, considers himself a "liberal" or not. But he compares Howard Stern with talk radio as if political talk radio were nothing more than shock-jocks. (Listeners know I'm not a big fan of everyone who passes himself off as a conservative radio show host, but none of them deserve to be associated with Howard Stern's style; that is simply wrong.)

Johnson also praises Obama, so he certainly counts as a liberal in my book. He also considers some of my opinions (as he has heard them) to be "odious and ill-informed." I can safely say there is no love lost between us.

Nevertheless, Johnson was mortified that I had been banned by the Home Office saying, "it just makes us look so infantile, so pathetic." It offended Johnson that the British people were treated as if they had to be protected from me. "What are we, some sort of kindergarten that needs to be protected against these dangerous American radio shows?" And he thought it was "blindingly obvious" that just because one disagreed strongly with me, one should still find it "very odd indeed to bar him from this country." Mr. Johnson went on to say:

> Perhaps Jacqui Smith thinks that it "sends out a signal" about the kind of Britain we want. On the contrary, it reinforces a culture–created by this Labour Government, and its addiction to political correctness–where people are increasingly confused and panic-stricken about what they can say and what is forbidden... Our courts and tribunals are clogged with people claiming to have suffered insults of one kind or another, and a country once famous for free speech is now hysterically and expensively sensitive to anything that could be taken as a slight.

This is truly a nightmare situation. And it surprises me that more liberals don't see how much it cuts against everything they claim to stand for. I'm glad Johnson saw the problem and wrote about it.

It is not just liberal writers, however.

I've always been an Anglophile (until recent events perhaps!) but I've also always known the country is more liberal than the US and the majority of the population is more liberal. Furthermore, even though as a democracy they need free speech, they don't actually have a First Amendment as we do in the US. But even so, the vast majority of this more liberal population believes I should be allowed to travel freely to and in their country if I want to do so. A *Daily Mail* online poll came out in England which said, "Should U.S. talk show host Michael Savage be banned from the U.K.? Only 21 percent said, "yes." Seventy-nine percent answered "no."

So, eight out of ten Brits say, "No, of course he shouldn't be banned." It is not so much the people of Britain who are to blame for what has happened to me. The survey indicates that the people in England have been hijacked by a government that represents the tiniest, smallest group of extremists in that country. This group of extremists has elected a government in Labour that has put the people themselves in prison, the prison of England.

Fox Fumbles

It's one thing for politicians to keep their distance from talk radio, but one would expect that the conservative media would show more concern for free speech and the threat of censorship. But that's not the case. In terms of American reaction to my being banned from the United Kingdom, perhaps the most stunning thing of all is the muted, and in some cases completely absent, voice of the so called conservative media. Some liberal news outlets even did better!

One thing that has interested me immensely about the reaction to my being banned from England is the fact that true liberals, not the neo-Marxist dreck that the liberal movement has descended into, were actually on my side. The far-left Jon Stewart, on *The Daily Show*, made a powerful argument through satire that Britain was dead-wrong to have put me on the list.

CNN, to their credit and in spite of their far-left bias, picked up on the story almost immediately. Lou Dobbs in particular did himself a rare bit of justice by examining the incident in a truly fair and balanced way. Liberal newspaper writers, bloggers, and columnists from across the world and the country, seemed to recognize better than many so-called conservatives, that my inclusion on the list was a dangerous thing indeed.

Certainly there were many neo-Marxist holdouts, such as those on MSLGBT who couldn't see past their own lifestyles, and therefore concluded that because they disagreed with Michael Savage, his being shut out of an entire nation was a good thing. But as with so many of their views, their conclusion is a suicidal one.

I suppose they never got around to reading that famous poem by Pastor Martin Niemöller. A German during the Nazi regime, he movingly encapsulated the apathy of the people, including himself, as Hitler gained more power:

> When the Nazis came for the communists,
> I remained silent;
> I was not a communist.
> Then they locked up the social democrats,
> I remained silent;
> I was not a social democrat.
> Then they came for the trade unionists,
> I did not protest;
> I was not a trade unionist.
> Then they came for the Jews,
> I did not speak out;
> I was not a Jew.
> When they came for me,
> There was no one left to speak out for me.

First they come for the conservative talk show hosts, and you do not speak up because you are not a conservative talk show host. But as the poem goes, by the time they come to you liberals, there is no one left to speak up for you.

But most liberals actually seem to have understood what a serious threat this is to our political system—and to free speech around the world. And because of that, I think there is real hope. Not the kind of false hope that is spread by Barack Hussein Obama. Not the kind of hope that is predicated on giving trillions of dollars to fraudsters, but the kind of hope that comes from seeing different people with different points of view unite because they realize that the differences they have with each other are small in comparison to the threat from those either here or in England who would impose a dictatorship of thought.

While the reaction of many American liberals has been gratifying and surprising, not so for the so-called conservative media in the United States.

Fox News–the "last bastion of conservative media"–refused to pick up on the story for days. In the immediate aftermath of my being banned, one show after another on this so-called conservative network refused to mention the name of Michael Savage or even address this gross violation of freedom of speech in even the most cursory way on their cable news channel.

After three days, the silence was broken by Bill O'Reilly, *aka* the leprechaun, who grudgingly took on the story, I'm sure only after receiving numerous e-mails from outraged listeners, some of whom copied me on their angry remarks to him. And when he did take up the story, he did everything possible to avoid talking about me, even though I was at the heart of the story.

This egotistical attitude would be laughable if it weren't so sad. What Bill O'Reilly doesn't seem to understand is that, regardless of our petty squabbles, everyone in the media–conservatives, liberals, moderates and extremists–are threatened by what happened to me. Today it might be Michael Savage, but tomorrow it could be Bill O'Reilly, or Rush Limbaugh, who also seems to have completely ignored the issue. The same is true of Sean Hannity. While many other hosts that included Rusty Humphries, Jerry Doyle, Mike Gallager, Joyce Kaufman and Lars Larson expressed full-throated outrage that England would attack free speech in this manner, neither of the top two hosts in the nation were willing to touch it.

I can only guess that for them, egos are bigger than issues.

But I'm not the only one to notice the silence of Fox News and others. One law professor wrote,

> Where is the outrage from the big-named conservative media giants like Fox News, Rush, Hannity, Mike Gallagher, Scarborough, Laura Ingraham, Monica Crowley, Dr. Laura Schlessinger, O'Reilly, Cavuto, Glenn Beck, Greta, National Review, Weekly Standard, Human Events, American Enterprise Institute and The Hoover Institute? Other than one unremarkable short TV segment by

O'Reilly and two excellent short stories by Bret Baier at Fox News, there is only the vexing sound of crickets chirping. With the exception of Joseph Farah's *WorldNetDaily*, I cannot cite a single media entity, think-tank or radio host in America that has dedicated themselves to preserving this vital story and keeping it alive with rigorous and trenchant analysis.[9]

But the mystery of silence can't be explained by pointing a finger at one or two personalities. We are talking about a whole network here! Why is Fox News–this allegedly conservative network, this allegedly "fair and balanced" network–so silent about a free speech issue that would seem to represent a threat against them as well? One can only wonder what their reaction would have been if Hannity or Bill O'Reilly had been the target of the Labour Home Office's ban.

It absolutely boggles the mind!

After all, I write this as one having been attacked by the media, both by the Democrats and by the Republicans. Last year, after I won the Freedom of Speech Award, C-SPAN refused to air my speech, and then C-SPAN's Brian Lamb attacked my listeners on the air.

Then Republican Senator Trent Lott told the New York Times, "Talk radio is running America and we have to deal with that problem." He said this for the simple reason that voters, informed by talk radio, were making it difficult for him to get his way with the Amnesty Bill for illegal aliens. He shamelessly attacked talk radio listeners and advocated ignoring voters. He said, "I'm sure senators on both sides of the aisle are being pounded by these talk-radio people who don't even know what's in the bill,"(which was not only untrue, but really describes the work of Congress on Obama's "stimulus" bill. These people think nothing of voting for legislation they have not read, but attack others as ignorant). He asserted that the Senate would work against the will of the people, saying that "leadership will have to be prepared to do what needs to be done."[10]

It was about that same time that there were reports that Hillary Clinton and Barbara Boxer were, years earlier, overheard plotting to develop a "legislative fix" for talk radio in an attempt to put me, Michael Savage, out of business.

But are these truly independent voices, attacking Michael Savage and talk radio from all parts of the political spectrum, or is there something that ties these voices together? Does the fact that Rupert Murdoch hosted a fundraiser for Hillary Clinton in 2006 mean anything? Or the fact that Murdoch's company, NewsCorp, paid Trent Lott $250,000 to write a book that sold 12,000 copies?

And what about the fact that C-SPAN receives funding from cable companies, and satellite services such as DirecTV, which has 15 million subscribers and is 34 percent owned by NewsCorp? Brian Lamb claims that C-SPAN is not funded by taxpayers…

> We are not a taxpayer organization. We have told our audience that many, many times. We get no federal funds, state funds, local funds. We get our money from you. You give us a nickel a month when you pay your bills, and that's how we operate here.

How disingenuous—not to mention downright dishonest. All cable companies have to maintain an FCC license, and C-SPAN lobbies for the requirement that these companies keep C-SPAN afloat with a portion of their revenue. It is all one state-corporate, corporate-state mixture.

Are these independent voices? Are these legitimate criticisms? Or are Trent Lott, Hillary Clinton, and Brian Lamb all tentacles of a greater power that is determined to wipe out talk radio, to silence Michael Savage and others like him, to end all independent thought in the United States of America?

The forces of darkness are gathering to try and blot out the truth. Those who pull the strings of our leaders and the media are out to destroy anyone who would dare oppose them. I have told you again and again about the Government-Media Complex, and now we see again how it operates. The puppet masters pull their corporate strings, and the empty suits and empty skirts and our so-called leaders dance to their tune. Fox News is part of the problem, not part of the solution.

And so today, since the people have been roused by the evil talk radio hosts, you'll hear the cable channels talk about Paris Hilton instead of illegal immigration. You'll hear about fires in Tahoe instead of fires in Baghdad. You'll hear about Tom Cruise instead of cruise missiles. Distraction is destruction. They have launched an all-out attack against reality.

Fight back! Let the truth be heard! Ungag talk radio! And let them know that *The Savage Nation* is listening and will not be silenced!

In this context, I found it was the smaller talk show hosts who came to my defense. Miami's Joyce Kaufman, for example, was outraged on my behalf.

> When I learned that Dr. Michael Savage had been banned from entering the U.K. I had two reactions. The first one was visceral, "I'm as mad as hell and I'm not going to take this anymore."… The second reaction was disgust.
>
> What happened to our great British allies? When did they abdicate the very principles on which great countries have led the world? When did they decide that the truth was irrelevant and the enemies of freedom needed to be placated? And more importantly, when did we become so tolerant of the politically incorrect cabal worldwide? Not on my watch, not in my country!
>
> There is a great scene in the movie "Spartacus" where the Roman Legion asks the revolting gladiators to identify and turn over their leader, Spartacus. And one by one they stood to their feet and denied the authorities a chance to easily identify him. So today I declare, *I am Michael Savage*. Do you stand with us for freedom of speech, or is this the end of the free world as we know it?[11]

Several others spoke up. Rusty Humphries of the Talk Radio Network said that he had "witnessed firsthand the hate speech not only tolerated but encouraged by the U.K." and was "appalled and amused at the suggestion that Michael Savage is banned from the U.K. for his speech." His reaction was clear: "Thank God we broke away from that cowardly country."[12]

"Although I am sorry to see the depths to which a once great nation like the U.K. has fallen, I cannot say that I am surprised," said Steve Malzberg, a New York talker on WOR. He described Britain as "a country which cares more about protecting and appeasing radical Muslims than it does about protecting its people and promoting free speech and free thought." He worried, however, about how the policies in that country might affect our own.

> I fear that this will now be added to the arsenal of the free speech fascists in the United States who are about to unleash their unprece-

dented attack on all of us. I look for Obama himself to eventually make note of it, in support of the action of course. All of us, who do what Michael does, need to make this issue number one.[13]

Several others also spoke up, including Lars Larson, Roger Hedgecock, Steve Gill, and Rev. Jesse Lee Peterson.

Listeners Rally

Getting banned from Britain was revealing. I found out who my real friends were and I found out who weren't. There are people within my inner circle who I will never speak to again because they weren't there for me when I needed them. I discovered certain members of my family who were so sick and jealous that I will never speak to them again. On the other hand, I had a friend with whom I'd had a falling out with a year earlier. He came to my aid and we became friends again. You know, crises bring people together and crises drive people apart.

While some friends and family were unwilling to help in my time of need, there were strangers far and wide coming to my rescue. As the word of my being banned from Britain spread around the world, thousands of individuals began to come to my defense.

Most surprising was the reaction of the British themselves. I've already mentioned British support for free speech, but this went beyond that. I have received incredible support, both for me and for my message. For example, I received a copy of the following letter from a British expatriate to Jacqui Smith:

Dear Madam,

I am a British National... I currently reside in Los Angeles, California in the United States as a Green Card Holder and have lived here for eleven years. In the eleven years as a resident of California I listen to Dr. Michael Savage's talk radio show every day if possible.

I can categorically state that I agree with every opinion, belief and notion Dr. Savage has expressed through his radio show, written word and articles. I have made financial donations to his Freedom of Speech Legal Fund and will continue to do so and have bought a number of his bestselling books.

I am a practicing Catholic who strongly believes in the right to bear arms under the United States Constitution although I am not permitted to own a fire arm under U.S. Law as a Resident Alien. I am a member of the RNC... I am a strong anti-abortion advocate and have attended many protests outside abortion clinics in Houston, TX and here in California.

I am totally opposed to illegal immigration here in the U.S. and the United Kingdom. ...[I]t is my belief that there is a faction of fanatical Muslims inciting violence in the United Kingdom who wish to overthrow the government of Great Britain. I strongly object to liberalism and oppose the Labor Government and the Democratic Government of the United States.

As a result of Dr. Michael Savage's ban on entering the U.K. due to being put on a "Least Wanted" list by yourself, I would like to know if the British Government will revoke my Passport and deny me entry to the U.K. due to my affiliation to Dr. Savage and as my thoughts and beliefs are aligned with his.

I demand an immediate response to my enquiry and furthermore demand your resignation as Home Secretary with a stipulation of a written apology on behalf of the British people to Dr. Savage. I will be making a financial contribution to Dr. Savage's legal fund in the lawsuit of defamation against yourself and your affiliates.

You have brought shame and embarrassment to me personally as a British citizen and I will make it my mission to see that you and your ilk are brought to justice to the full extent to the law.

This email came from an Englishman still living in the country:

> Hello Michael.
> Just a few lines to say that I had never heard of you before my corrupt government banned you from entering England (of course the rest of the third world can come). But now I go daily to your web site for straight from the hip comment. Keep up the good work because we have nothing like you on our airways.

Clearly, not all Brits believed the lies about Michael Savage that the British government was telling them. I even got an e-mail from a cruise-ship company. "Dear Michael Savage," it said...

> "Just a thought about Great Britain. I am more than happy to facilitate a New York to London transatlantic cruise and conference to test the backbone of the Hetero-phobic, pro-Islamic, anti-Judeo Christian, pseudo-tolerant Brits...Hope you are doing well."

It would be very interesting to have fifteen-hundred individuals on a Michael Savage Freedom of Speech Tour to England, and the ship was not permitted to dock at South Hampton. Do you think the Brits would turn away all that money? Do you think the Brits would turn away all that foreign currency?

Of course, many in the United States came to stand up with me–like Pastor James Manning. And out of nowhere, a man from Los Angeles spoke out for me at a meeting of the L.A. City Council. Here are his words as they entered the public record:

> I'm a proud member of the Savage Nation. A proud member of the Savage Nation. Every day at 3:00 I am honored and thrilled to listen to every single word that comes out of Michael Savage's mouth. I agree with 120% of what Michael Savage says.
>
> Why am I here this morning? Because the Home Secretary of England has banned Michael Savage from entering England. I'm calling on the L.A. City Council this morning to pass a resolution supporting the right of Michael Savage to say what he wants. You

don't have to listen to him anymore than I have to listen to you. But Michael Savage represents millions of Americans. You're looking at one right now.

You know, Tom–and Jack Weiss–you're my councilmen and you're my neighboring councilman, Jack Weiss. You know Michael Savage is a big supporter of Israel and the Jewish people. He is not a racist. He's not a homophobe. He's not a hater. Everything that Michael Savage has said is right.

I think that this council will set history. The whole country will be looking to this council if you pass a motion supporting the right of Michael Savage to enter the country of England. He brings you a lot of money to the city of L.A. Many people that live in the city of L.A. might be next.

I used to be on the radio on the same station as Michael Savage. I, too, am a Jew. I, too, am a broadcaster. I don't want to be denied the right to travel to England because of my political points of view. So, Michael lives up in San Francisco. The SF City Council will never pass this kind of resolution. But I am asking you to please pass a resolution supporting Michael Savage. I can't wait until 3:00 today. Liberals and mental disorders–will be confirmed. Thank you.

He talked to a few of the councilmen afterwards. They said to him, "There's nothing we can do."

But people all over the country can do this at their local city councils.

I have received other support as well, and many letters of support have been sent to me. One letter came to me from a gentleman in Far Rockaway, New York, who wrote to the British Consul General, 845 Third Ave., NY, NY 10022:

I put you on notice that the stench from this woman's mouth radiates to destroy our First Amendment here in the U.S.A. This low-life, Jacqui Smith, mirrors the Nazis in the 1930s, destroying Europe by putrid propaganda.

Your country was practically destroyed and put to the grave because of the rats that roamed the British Parliament in the 1930s. America's free speech, free expression saved you from the grave. Evidently since you did not dispute this low-life rat, Jacqui Smith, you agree as to her expression.

I am a World War II veteran and I am so sorry that I fought to save your behind. This ranting gutter snipe Jacqui Smith, expressing her hatred of Michael Savage, allows terrorists in your country who will eventually take it over. Your Great Britain as mirrored by Winston Churchill is no more. The question arises, "who in my country or in Washington DC" induced this witch lunatic in England to put Michael Savage on this list?

People in America should boycott any travel to Great Britain or purchase anything made in Great Britain.

Thank you.

And this message from one of my sponsors was particularly encouraging:

Call me crazy, but I had a dream last night about you, Michael. The long and short is what happened to you with this attack from the nutcase in England. While very painful and burdensome, it ultimately saved the nation of England. You singlehandedly awoke a nation out of its slumber and people listened to you like never before. You were then not only heralded as a national treasure in America but Great Britain as well. The dream was so real I woke up and had to grab the nightstand to assure myself the world around me was real and it was just a dream. Hang in there!

I have every intention of "hanging in there!" I can't deny that it gets hard, but letters of support and encouragement are a great help. I've found that I have many co-belligerents in this battle, and I appreciate every single person who has written to express their support.

The Loyal Savage Bloggers

Of course, for news like this to break in this day and age entails an immediate explosion of Internet activity. As one rather liberal writer–one who still believes in free speech–explains,

> Quite predictably, the most likely outcome of this debacle is that Savage would get instantaneous name recognition beyond the United States, with audiences on both sides of the Atlantic having to listen to his...sound bites.... A host of conservative and Internet-savvy bloggers are already wasting a lot of bandwidth to rally behind the man. There was also a noticeable spike in Savage-driven Twitter conversations: according to Twist, a Twitter-tracking service, discussions about Savage made up around 0.05% of all Twitter discussions on May 6th, shortly after the British decision was announced.[14]

It was more than just Twitter, though. Websites and blogs were full of references to me after this happened. Of course, the mainstream conservative blogosphere was almost as bad as Fox News. *National Review Online*'s blog, "The Corner," said almost nothing, and then made sure to be dismissive when briefly mentioning what had happened. One writer, however, who has struggled with censorship himself in the form of the Canadian "human rights" court for telling the truth about Islamic terrorism, was quick to respond with more defense of me (and with no disdain). He wrote,

> The British Home Secretary thinks that by making public the ban on Michael Savage she's "naming and shaming" him. But she's shaming only herself and her country. This kind of stuff is very weird from a senior cabinet minister of a G7 nation.[15]

He then quoted the British government's self-righteous excuses for banning me invoking alleged "standards and values." He asks,

> How many members of King Abdullah's entourage at the G20 summit the other week live by Jacqui Smith's "standards and values"?

Come to that, how many British subjects live by the "standards and values" of the countries they visit and trade with? The idea of ideological enforcement at the border is repugnant to a free society.[16]

Truly conservative bloggers came to my defense as well. The *Desert Conservative* posted by Lisa Richards spoke directly to the charge that I could incite violence. "Savage has never called for violence or extremism," she wrote. "I know this because I listen to his radio show every night. Savage does not incite brutal behavior; his rhetoric speaks the truth, never calling for harm." Richards also pointed out another part of the hypocrisy of the banning: "Liberals in his hometown of San Francisco constantly provoke and display aggressive assaults against conservatives and Christians. *They* are welcome in the UK."[17]

She also spelled out "how ironic" Britain's policy of tolerance and intolerance really is:

> The UK is now targeted by subway and bus-bombing Muslims marching in London streets chanting death to Great Britain and the West. Parliament does nothing to Muslims; acting against the inciters of bloodshed would insult Islam...

> Michael Savage however is a dangerous man. Be careful if you are on the same plane as he; the PhD scientist might talk to you about the greatness of freedom, civil rights and New York pizza while explaining the beauty of Brazilian rain forest botany. Oh yes, Dr. Savage is precariously treacherous.[18]

Richards followed this up with a second, longer post that served as a comprehensive defense of me against my British accuser. "Attacking Michael Savage is an assault against free speech and civil rights," she wrote, "Placing Savage's name on a list with murderers, making false allegations against him, violates his rights."[19]

Perhaps the longest and most detailed defense in the blogosphere came from the American Thinker blog. This was not a fan blog, by any means, but rather provides a news journal in cyberspace.

Nevertheless, investigative journalist Peter Barry Chowka wrote a serious piece that showed me to be the victim of a government that has no respect for free speech. It also recorded the media apathy toward me that helped Britain's Home Office get away with banning me.[20]

There were many other defenders as well, including fans at the *Free Republic* website (www.freerepublic.org).

Savage Keeps the Faith

Naturally, I could not acquiesce to what was happening to me. It was tempting in some ways to simply "hide"–to complain on my radio show but not do much else. After all, how does one take on an entire nation's government? How could I fight when the most powerful voices were not going to speak on my behalf even when their own well-being was, in principle, threatened?

But I knew I could not do that. I had to fight this, not only for my own sake, but for others. This entailed several different struggles. First, of course, I had to raise awareness through my show and every other means of communication that I could find. I had to do all I could to recruit others to spread the news of what is happening in Britain and in the U.S. as well.

But it could not stop there. I also had to pursue both every political and legal avenue possible to get my name off that list. I would need to raise funds to carry on that immense battle.

I resolved to do all it would take. I am still resolved to do so!

I have a dream…

> *I have a dream that one day free men and women will be judged not on their correctness of their political views, but on the content of their character. I have a dream that all the mindless mandarins that plague the body politicks in all nations will be driven out of all their little cubicles in all massive faceless government buildings around the world. I have a dream that they will be made to answer for all the vile petty judgments that they have placed on others. That they will be called to account for all the careers and livelihoods that they have taken away. That they will reap the just rewards of all the suicidal insanity that they have sown.*

I have a dream that one day, all the people of the world will rise up and throw off the shackles that small minded malcontents have placed on them, and that they will be free to enjoy the fruits of their own labor, and their own ideas in a way they best see fit. I have a dream that one day I will sail a ship filled with such men and women, those with free and open minds, on the same route over the Atlantic Ocean taken by American convoys as they went to resupply the British in World War Two and fortify them against the Nazi menace. I have a dream that this ship will land in England, dock in England, and I will set foot on British soil, and say, "Tear down this wall that you have placed before me. Tear down this wall against freedom of speech."

And I have a dream that then the people of England, inspired by the freedoms of the Magna Carta, will stand up, tear down the emerging wall of totalitarianism, and declare with one voice: "This is the land of Freedom once more."

Chapter Notes

[1] James Slack and Nicola Boden, "Jacqui Smith's latest disaster: Banned U.S. shock jock never even tried to visit Britain - now he's suing, *Daily Mail*, May 7, 2009, http://www.dailymail.co.uk/news/article-1177428/Jacqui-Smiths-latest-disaster-Banned-U-S-shock-jock-tried-visit-Britain--hes-suing.html (Last viewed July 23, 2009).

[2] Lester Haines, "Wacky Jacqui defends Michael Savage ban," *The Register* (May 19, 2009), http://www.theregister.co.uk/2009/05/19/jacqui_smith_savage/ (Seen on July 13, 2009).

[3] Ibid.

[4] Ibid.

[5] "Britain's ban of Savage decried by detractors," *The San Francisco Chronicle*, May 6, 2009, http://www.sfgate.com/cgibin/article.cgi?f=/c/a/2009/05/05/ MN3617FA8K.DTL (Last viewed on July 23, 2009).

[6] Ibid.

[7] Evgeny Morozov, "The Savage effect triggers a viral tsunami," *Foreign Policy*, May 10, 2009. http://neteffect.foreignpolicy.com/posts/2009/05/10/the_savage_effect_triggers_a_viral_tsunami (Last viewed on July 21, 2009).

[8] "Michael Savage poses no risk to British security so why won't MPs say so?" May 10, 2009, http://www.telegraph.co.uk/comment/columnists/borisjohnson/5304788/Michael-Savage-poses-no-risk-to-British-security-so-why-wont-MPs-say-so.html

[9] Ellis Wahington, "The Savage Silence of the Lambs," *World Net Daily*, May 20, 2009. http://www.wnd.com/index.php?fa=PAGE.view&pageId=98604 (Last viewed on August 5, 2009).

[10] Jonathan Weisman and William Branigin, "Bush Continues Push for New Immigration Bill," *Washington Times*, June 15, 2007, http://www.washington post.com/wpdyn/content/article/2007/06/15/AR2007061500843_pf.html (Last viewed on July 23, 2009).

[11] "Savage's colleagues react in horror," *World Net Daily*, May 5, 2009, http://www.wnd.com/index.php?fa=PAGE.view&pageId=97136 (Last viewed on July 23, 2009).

[12] Ibid.

[13] Ibid.

[14] Evgeny Morozov, "The Savage effect triggers a viral tsunami," *Foreign Policy,* May 10, 2009. http://neteffect.foreignpolicy.com/posts/2009/05/10/ the_savage_effect_triggers_a_viral_tsunami (Last viewed on July 21, 2009).

[15] Mark Steyn, "Re: Just For the Record," NRO blog: The Corner, May 6, 2009, http://corner.nationalreview.com/post/ ?q=Y2Q4YWY3NzdkYzI5Yz NhNWJlMzNjM2QwNjY3MDJmNzU= (Last viewed July 23, 2009).

[16] Ibid.

[17] "America LEFT England for a REASON: Uncompassionate Savage Treatment" *Desert Conservative*, July 2, 2009, http://www.desertconservative. com /2009/07/02/america-left-england-for-a-reason/ (Viewed July 23, 2009).

[18] Ibid.

[19] Lisa Richards, Exclusive: Michael Savage Banned From Great Britain: The Crime? Speaking His Mind, *Family Security Matters,* July 11, 2009, http://www.familysecuritymatters.org/publications/id.3719/pub_detail.asp (Last viewed on July 22, 2009).

[20] Peter Barry Chowka, Michael Savage Banned in the UK, *American Thinker*, May 10, 2009, http://www.americanthinker.com/2009/05/ michael_savage_banned_in_the_u.html (Last viewed on July 23, 2009).

6

Change to Bereave In:
How Did We Get Here?

The United States is in trouble. The West is in trouble. So far this book has dealt with an American citizen being publicly libeled and banned by a foreign government. This government is supposed to be at peace with, and even a friend of, the United States. Britain attacked me because they wanted a white, conservative, non-Muslim, to treat as a threat. They wanted to deny that the British government was trying to deal with terrorists who are Islamic. The United States government itself says and does nothing about the libel or ban.

Furthermore, that same American government is moving to intimidate political speech using law enforcement and the false excuse of terrorism. Like the British government, it too seems intent on putting out the message that we are not facing a unique threat in Islamic terrorism. Like the British government, it too is singling out conservatives to do so.

All of these things are part of a larger picture. It is not, I repeat *not*, a picture that was drawn only by Obama and his backers. This is not something that can be legitimately blamed only on the Democrats. It started much earlier than Obama's rise to power.

The Republicans in power had to first decide to give him the country.

Multi-Cultural Globalism and Its Discontents

After it was revealed that I was selected by the Home Office to "balance" their list of Islamic murderers and convicts, a blogger on religion for the UK's *The Telegraph*, Ed West, observed:

Savagegate is the latest example of the Labour Government's refusal to recognize that the only real threat to our country is from Muslim terrorists. They have gone out of their way–with the help of the BBC, which almost never mentions the *I*-word whenever some loser gets caught with bomb-making equipment–to deny that Islamic terrorism, while not supported by most British Muslims, is still Islamic.

Jacqui Smith, whose experience as a schoolteacher did not extend to serious Koranic scholarship as far as anyone knows, even re-branded Islamic terrorism as "anti-Islamic activity". She said of the attacks on London and Glasgow in 2007: "Indeed, if anything, these actions are anti-Islamic." As far as I know they never referred to neo-Nazi terrorists organizing "anti-white activity," but then those trained in Marxist politics can be selective when applying "false consciousness."[1]

What this means is that it isn't realistic to separate domestic policy and civil liberties from foreign policy and national security. The same delusional and dangerous multi-cultural or "politically correct" ethos brings tyranny and censorship to both areas. Refusing to deal with Islamofascism abroad means enforcing fascism at home in order to make room for it. Opening the borders to all sorts of illegals, including national-security threats to the nation, means needing to find ways to marginalize and silence those who want the government to do its job.

Ed West's observations about what is going on in Britain are not so different than what is happening, or soon to happen, in the United States. By "denying the religious motivation" of terrorist groups, he writes, "the Government has pandered to the Muslim sense of grievance which, like the related Arab sense of 'humiliation,' is totally unjustified and fed by self-hating western liberals."[2] I believe he is right, and that the self-hatred, in turn, translates into hatred of others–not of Muslim terrorists, but of conservatives who don't buy into the self-loathing that liberals have decided is the mark of civilized human beings. "Rather than explaining honestly that the only reason mosques and Muslim groups are investigated by MI5 is because there are no Jews or Christians trying to attack this country," West continues, "the Government tries to deny the theological nature of the terrorists, and to desperately find non-Muslims to threaten us." Even though he is talking about Britain, he clearly explains what is going on with the Department of Homeland Security doing all it can to spread suspicion of conservatives as a terrorist threat and to energize law enforcement agencies on all levels to harass them.

This refusal to truly admit to the real threats America faces is dangerous to the nation but provides profits to some. America is on the brink of destruction. North Korea is threatening us with nukes. Iran is next in line. China is crushing us economically. Illegal aliens are crushing us economically. And what is our leadership saying? Forget about Obama for a moment and go back to Bush. "There will be serious consequences." "We will impose sanctions." "We need free trade." "We need guest workers."

Pabulum, promises, appeasement, and passivity.

Our leadership was and is nowhere. Our leadership was and is weak. Our leadership sold us out because our leadership would rather watch our nation be destroyed from within and without than lose a single dollar in profit from their globalist machinations. Lenin said, "We will hang the last capitalist with the rope he sells us." While Lenin was responsible for the deaths of millions, and while he created one of the greatest threats to our way of life and brainwashed generations of the weak-minded, he may have spoken the truth in this one case.

Why don't we attack North Korea's nuclear sites? We are distracted by lucrative contracts in Iraq. Why don't we pressure China to act with massive tariffs? We are too addicted to their cheap goods. Why don't we close the border? Illegals are easier to hire than welfare recipients and too many politicians see future voters to exploit.

When the bottom line is payoffs, not patriotism, we are in serious trouble. When the bottom line is contracts instead of country, we are in dark times. When the bottom line is assets instead of action, we are on the verge of seeing our nation destroyed. Too many nests are being feathered. Too many palms are being greased. We need to drive the money-changers from the temple of our nation before they and the madman from Korea, the madman from Iran, and the madmen from Washington DC destroy it.

This has been my message for a long time–even before George Bush and Henry Paulson started looting the American people for the sake of the wealthy in Manhattan. Even before they set the precedent for nationalizing industries and turning us into a socialist state that, as Churchill warned, could no longer "afford to allow free, sharp, or violently worded expressions of public discontent," I saw this day coming.

The Last Days of Bush: From Kyoto to Bushito

As his second term progressed, and even during his first term to some extent, Bush destroyed his own conservative base a little more with every passing day. At the time I am writing this, the news is full of stories (usually Obama puff pieces) about the draconian measure "Cap and Trade" bill that will be a body-blow to our economy and kill off what manufacturing we still have in this country. Of course, even if it is defeated, the EPA can still autonomously punish industry in all sorts of ways in the name of protecting us from climate change.

But it was the Bush Administration that started this process–not Obama! Back in the summer of 2007, at the G8 Summit, Bush agreed, in principle, to stringent restrictions on carbon dioxide emissions–cutting 1990 levels in half.[3] While pundits and activists were full of scorn, claiming that Bush was not really on board with the G8 resolutions, they were sadly wrong.

On April 16, 2008, Bush followed up by ending what resistance he had shown to the dangerous and unnecessary environmentalist agenda and gave a speech announcing that we would pursue "stabilization" in so-called "greenhouse gas" emissions and eventually global reductions. Having resisted the Kyoto Protocol because it was so damaging, he opened the door to legitimize the same sorts of restrictions!

The media was full of reports saying that Bush's change was not nearly enough. That may have comforted conservatives. But the change represented a real danger to the American economy because it legitimized the entire environmentalist program. As the *Christian Science Monitor* reported, even though it wasn't "environmentalist" *enough*, it at least served as "a strong acknowledgment of a need for action."

The speech President Bush delivered in the Rose Garden Wednesday afternoon has resonated even with people who find many of its details wanting.

"Given the administration's track record and its reputation on global climate-change policy to date, this is a step in the right direction," says Robert Stavins, an environmental economist at Harvard University.

The speech's significance, he adds, lies less with its implications for global warming than with its effect on "a substantial number of Republicans in the House and Senate who are on the fence," as Congress considers global warming legislation. The call for emissions goals could–especially if it were combined with acquiescence on some form of emissions-trading–help build GOP support for some of the measures Congress is considering, he says.[4]

So, even though there was more to be done, the war's outcome was now certain because Bush caved and undermined the position of any conservatives left in Congress! As in many other cases that we will see, the Obama Administration is simply building on what Bush started.

But it gets worse. Bush didn't wait for Obama. At the next G8 conference in northern Japan in July 2008, the President of the United States furthered his betrayal of his country and his conservative base for the sake of appearing respectable in the eyes of foreign powers. One day after reporting that Bush was "coming under strong pressure from the European Union and Japan" to make even more drastic cuts in carbon dioxide emission,[5] the UK's *Guardian* reported, "George Bush today paved the way *for his successor in the White House* to strike an historic deal on climate change"[6] that targeted cutting alleged "greenhouse" emission *at least* in half by 2050.

This put us further down the road the 2007 G8 summit had started upon.

That summer of 2007 was a time when we saw several other ways in which Bush served Globalism and rejected his own base. At that earlier G7 summit, the world was told that Bush was planning to give $60 billion in foreign aid to Africa, much of it directly from the US. This large commitment was reaffirmed in 2008.

Not only was this bad news for an economy that many knew was about to enter a global recession, but it actually is the kind of thing that has devastated Africa.[7]

Of course, the summer of 2007 was also when Bush again came to the defense of his massive amnesty bill and told the nation, "America must not fear diversity. We ought to welcome diversity."[8]

Did George Bush experience a crack-up? Who was at the helm of the ship of state? Bush's generals were saying we needed to fight a nicer war. His advisers accused those who dared to oppose him on the amnesty bill of national chauvinism. His allies in the Senate called conservatives, "bigots." His brother Jeb, and RNC head Ken Mehlman, claimed Republicans should have passed proposition 187 in California–which merely denied public services to illegal immigrants.[9]

What was the source of this madness? What party did Bush belong to?

The truth is that Bush belonged to no party. He was not on the side of the American people. He is on the side of KBR–an engineering company notorious for military contracts. He is on the side of those who want cheap labor and no jobs for real Americans. He is on the side of "diversity"–an ironic name for a policy and goal that requires suppressing dissent in order to be successful.

Earlier, in April of 2006, the Bush administration commended the Venezuelan public for participating in democracy, a *de facto* congratulation of Hugo Chavez on his election victory. Our politicians, even in the case of a Republican President, were patting socialists on the back. "Go, girl, go."

They were chummy with Communists, even as a red stain spread across our hemisphere. In that case, also, we saw that there was no conservative leadership. Once again, we were betrayed by those who claim to represent the American right. Just as when Bush held hands with the king of Saudi Arabia, this latest disappointment will probably be followed by a group hug with Chavez and Castro. Republicans made a great deal about Obama bowing to King Abdulla of Saudi Arabia, but that sort of posture, even if not so obvious, had already been assumed by the Republican President who preceded him.

If Bush can hold hands with Saudi Arabia while they buy bombs for the terrorists, if Bush can pat Hugo Chavez on the back after he calls him the devil, what other insanity is possible? Would Churchill have shared pasta fagioli with Mussolini? Would Roosevelt have had beer and bratwurst with Hitler while telling him how much he admired the efficiency of the German military, but he was going just a little too far on the Auschwitz thing? Is the fact that there is oil in Saudi Arabia and oil in Venezuela enough to make us forget the fact that we are a nation that hates evil, deplores Communism, and loves freedom? If we've moved from Saudi Sheik to Marxist Chic without a second thought, are we dead as a nation? We must stop braying to Mecca. We must stop bowing to Caracas. And until we do, we will be at the mercy of the throat-cutters, whether they are Islamofascists or Hispanocommunists. Whether Saudi Sheik or Marxist Chic, Bush should have been a warrior rather than a politician.

After 9/11, and when he first went into Iraq, we thought that George W. Bush represented Bushido, the old Japanese warrior code. We thought there was honor in the Bush administration. But we learned after awhile that there was none. Instead of Bushido, we have Bushito, which is code for destroying our borders, eliminating our culture, eviscerating the military, and selling out America.

One illustration of Bush's commitment to Globalism rather than nationalism can be seen in the movement of Halliburton. When Dubai tried to gain control of the United States port system, I spoke out on my radio program and the rest of the media followed me. The Islamofascists were stopped because *The Savage Nation* initially alerted America to the danger. But they have not given up. If Mohammed cannot come to the mountain, then Mohammed will force the mountain to come to him. And that is what has happened. In March 2007, Halliburton announced that it is moving its corporate headquarters to Dubai.

Yes, the company that made money off Vietnam, the company that made money off Clinton's killing in Kosovo, and the company that is helping to bleed us dry in Iraq is now pulling up stakes and moving to the Middle East. Answering the call to prayer of their Muslim masters, Halliburton, the company that in its various incarnations has employed George Bush's father, his grandfather, and Vice President Dick Cheney, has decided that the heart of the enemy is a better location to conduct business from than the good old U.S. of A.

For Halliburton, there is no United States. There is no such thing as national sovereignty. There is only the bottom line—the almighty dollar. If the pursuit of money means that Halliburton serves the Caliphate instead of the Impotentate George W. Bush, then that is fine with them.

When America was young, "Go West, young man" was the call that went out to those eager to blaze trails and forge a nation. Now that self-same nation is being dismantled under the banner of "Go East, young man." *Go East to drain your American blood. Go East to drain your American money. Go East to bray faithfully towards your masters in Mecca.*

Probably more key than any other factor in the ascendancy of Barack Obama is the fact that Republicans under George W. Bush abandoned real conservatism. During the Bush years, most people lost money. If you were a working American, your buying power was cut in half. If you made a hundred thousand dollars a year, you went to making fifty. If you made fifty thousand, you went to making twenty-five. Why is this? The reason is found in the Arab oil cartel in the Middle East, their friend the Hitler of Iran, and their fifth columnists in America, the oil company CEOs. What are the Democrats doing about it? Little. What are the Republicans doing about it? Nothing.

Once again we see that Republican politicians, though they claim to be conservatives, are usually nothing more than sellouts.

Take former Senator Phil Gramm. He ran as a conservative and was in the Senate for eighteen years. Did he close the borders during that time? Did he end the slaughter of children through abortion? Did he prevent our culture from rotting away into the cesspool we have today? No, no, and no. And what's worse, he didn't even try.

What he did do was gut the banking laws so his cronies in the financial industry could make more money at your expense. He supported free trade and sent our jobs to Mexico, and once he got out of the Senate, he took a nice cushy job as vice chairman of one of the banks whose pockets he helped to line.

Now, as the economy is falling apart thanks to the idiocy of the Bush administration and this Congress, former Senator Phil Gramm has called hard-working American citizens "whiners." The working man trying to support his family is a "whiner." The vet returning from Iraq trying to find a job that was outsourced is a "whiner." The cop on the beat who fights Mexican gangs but pays for their free healthcare with his taxes is a "whiner." Senator Phil Gramm should be tried for treason for what he's done to our country and for insulting the American people. He is the perfect illustration of the difference between Republicans and conservatives. Republicans claim to be conservatives, declare they will protect our borders, language and culture, and then when they get into office, they sell off to the corporate oligarchy. Conservatives aren't Democrats or Republicans–they're Independents. They're nationalists. They don't keep quiet when the Arabs try to screw us with $5 gas. They don't keep quiet when our politicians talk more about jobs in Columbia than jobs in the United States. And they don't keep quiet when traitors insult their intelligence.

The voices of those who call themselves conservative are propagandizing the airwaves. You can hear them saying there shouldn't be an FDA to protect us from salmonella, that illegal aliens are doing the jobs Americans won't do, and that attacking the minimum wage is anti-job. This is garbage. These people are globalist liberals masquerading as free marketers. They may be Republicans, but they are most definitely not conservatives. There's a huge difference between the two.

- Republicans are for AIDS money to Africa. Conservatives are for aid to working American citizens.

- Republicans are for bailing out billionaire money manipulators on Wall Street while you wait in line at the hospital behind an illegal alien. Conservatives are for letting Wall Street hucksters pay for their own mistakes and sending illegals back to Mexico.

- Republicans are for letting market forces decide if your food has fecal matter in it. Conservatives are for enforcing basic food safety standards so that Mexican farm workers can't crap in the fields and make you sick.

- Republicans think bringing in illegal aliens is an amnesty. Conservatives think bringing in illegal aliens is a travesty.

- Republicans want a strong global economy. Conservatives want a country.

- Republicans think that child porn on the internet is freedom from government. Conservatives know that smut is a poison that must be snuffed out.

America thought Bush was a conservative. He turned out to be just a Republican. And while there are Republicans who are conservatives, too, don't let the "R" after the name fool you. The voters knew the difference. And rather than vote for McCain, someone they knew was only pretending to be conservative; they either stayed home or voted for a man with charisma, even if they thought he would turn out to be a Marxist.

The Transformation of Barack and Michelle Obama

America has entered the Era of Obama. How did we get here? Much of what paved the way for Barack Obama to enter the White House was his campaign's success in transforming his image from that of a community activist into that of someone who was portrayed by the leftist media as a moderate. He was changed virtually overnight from a man whom even the left-wing *National Journal* called America's most liberal Senator. He became instead the savior of the country who even many Republicans could get behind.

Obama benefited from the media's turning the nation into the United States of Pravda. In the days of the Soviet Union, the official newspaper of the Communist government was called *Pravda. Pravda* is the Russian word for truth. Their articles would invariably follow the party line. No deviation from official state policy was ever tolerated. Today, although we have the appearance of a free media, complete with commentators, columnists and press conferences, what we have in fact is a state-run government media complex.

At every campaign stop by Barack Hussein Obama during the campaign, he went immediately to pre-selected reporters asking pre-selected questions. In every media appearance, questions that would have emphasized his far-left positions were glossed over because there is no free media in the United States of America. There is only a United States of Pravda. The government media complex clearly has a set of issues that it is not allowed to touch.

But it also has a set of people that it is not allowed to touch or criticize. In the ancient caste system of India, untouchables were the lowest order of society. But in the modern American media, the untouchables are the elite—those who aren't allowed to be criticized in any way, shape or form. The new untouchables include Barack Obama himself. It would be one thing to give a candidate the benefit of the doubt. To refuse to ask a single question about vital economic and national security issues was insane. To avoid pointing out that he wanted to talk to Iran and socialize the economy was not only stupid, ignorant, and sheepish, but traitorous. Because of it, Obama became a moderate instead of a Marxist.

The transformation of Michelle Obama was completed at the Democratic Convention. The speech she gave at the Convention was the same bland, hackneyed message that was expected of all Obama supporters at this convention. This is not the Michelle Obama we know. This is not the Michelle Obama who introduced her husband as "her baby's daddy." This is not the Michelle Obama who said she was proud of America for the first time in her life.

But if you think Michelle's handlers were worried she would be attacked for her race, you're wrong. Look at Bush's Secretary of State, Condoleeza Rice. Many conservatives and liberals disagreed with her, but there was never the same fundamental discomfort about her identity as there was with Michelle Obama. There's a fundamental difference between how Rice makes you feel and how Michelle Obama makes you feel. Rice, despite her politics and ineptitude, never evoked or projected anger or hostility. Michelle Obama does.

This is why the Democrats felt the need to transform her. All her rough edges were smoothed out. She talked about "public service" and "community volunteers" and "the American Dream." All the extremism was swept under the rug. All the far-left rhetoric was pushed to the side. All the extremists were kept out of the limelight. None of the political plankton was given a plank at this convention. Yet they reveal the true character of the Democrats.

Anyone who might have embarrassed the Obamas by their left-wing associations was kept away from the cameras and the microphones. This was why what viewers saw on television at the Democratic Convention was the modern equivalent of Soviet troops marching past Lenin's tomb. No dissidents. No disruptions. Just disinformation.

Time and time again, the leftist media came to the aid of Barack Obama. Perhaps the clearest example of this was when Obama was on the television show of former Clinton press secretary George Stephanopoulos. Obama referred to his "Muslim faith," a truth that all of the party apparatchiks and liberal talking heads in America haven't been able to cover up. Perhaps the most disgusting part of this entire incident is that as soon as Obama said the words "Muslim faith," the Democrat lackey George Stephanopoulos immediately jumped in and said, "Christian faith." The words "Muslim faith" came so naturally to him that Obama didn't even bother to correct himself. The left protects its own.

The question is this: How did he get this far? How did someone with an obviously Muslim background manage to become the anointed candidate of one of the two major parties in the United States of America? The answer is this–by the collusion of the media. The media covered up this inconvenient truth about Barack Hussein Obama because it did not fit into their storyline of the heroic black presidential candidate who would save America from its evil racist past. The media used his race as an excuse to support him and they simply refused to look any deeper than that.

America had a choice between an ex-Navy pilot and a community activist. It was a choice between someone who shot rockets at our enemies in battle and someone who shot staples into a telephone poll. Yet thanks in part to the assistance of the leftist media, America chose Barack Hussein Obama.

But the leftist media wasn't the only force on Obama's side. It seemed that at every turn, his so-called opponent, John McCain, was there to help him. McCain threw the election. It was clear with his choice for Vice President that McCain had no desire to win. Why else would he have chosen an inexperienced woman, whose only apparent qualification is that she won a beauty pageant in the 1980s? Why else would he have refused to say Barack Hussein Obama's middle name? Why else would he have run an ad praising Obama and congratulating him for winning the nomination?

If McCain had chosen Mitt Romney, a man with real leadership ability, real charisma, and real experience, he might have stood a chance. He could have made up for his lack of energy in confronting his opponent, his useless pandering to liberals, and his refusal to expose Obama's leftism and inexperience. Instead, he trumped inexperience with more inexperience. Obama, for all his neo-Marxism, picked a running mate who was perceived as giving the ticket more experience. McCain, in defiance of all logic, undermined his strong suit by selecting a political neophyte who watered down his key advantage over Obama. I was attacked during the campaign for coming out against Palin. Callers told me,

"Mike, you should give her a chance, she's a real conservative." They said, "Mike, he's just doing this because he knows he has to pander to win." "Mike," they said, "isn't it great that he picked a woman."

All these lockstep Republicans could not have been more wrong. Picking someone because of their sex instead of their ability is the same kind of affirmative action insanity that the Democrats try to shove down our throats. We didn't want a panderer; we wanted a president.

If McCain had chosen a woman who was a real nationalist with a real resume, I would have said, "Right on, John." But McCain dropped the ball, threw in the towel, and raised the white flag. Now a generation of Americans is paying for his stupidity.

The campaign showed the American people that the Democrat Party and the Republican Party serve no other purpose than the accumulation of power. There was a time when Democrats stood for true civil rights. That time has passed. There was a day when the Republicans stood for borders, language, and culture. That day is also over.

In fact, the Republican Convention and its aftermath showed us how both parties will engage in political cross-dressing. Once Sarah Palin was selected as John McCain's running mate, the Democrats developed overnight a deep concern over the propriety of teenage motherhood. At the same time, the Republicans suddenly said that if you question whether teenage motherhood is good for America, you must be a sexist. In 24 hours, the Republicans discarded 150 years of morality because they thought it would help them gain power. In a single day, the Democrats discovered morality because they thought it would help them take the Republicans down. It was the most absurd display of politics our country had ever seen.

The two-party system is morally bankrupt. Here's what George Washington had to say about it. "It serves to distract the Public Councils, and enfeeble the Public Administration... agitates the Community with ill-founded jealousies and false alarms; kindles the animosity of one....against another....it opens the door to foreign influence and corruption...thus the policy and the will of one country are subjected to the policy and will of another."

Over 200 years ago George Washington, our first president, knew that we would come to this point. So don't pretend that your party is fighting power for principal. They are fighting principally for power.

Regardless of who had won the election in 2008, we knew we were getting someone in the pockets of the puppet masters. The media told us again and again that Obama was a liberal and McCain was a conservative. Obama was for big government and McCain was for small government. Obama was for change, but McCain had the experience.

Yet when the American people, through their representatives in Congress, rejected the bailout and made it known they did not want to give another penny to Wall Street, these two candidates for president *both* supported the bailout. But the media claimed they were so different. How could this have happened?

The Era of Obama

The era of Obama means trickle-up poverty. Much of his financial insanity (as well as Bush's) will be covered in the next chapter. But we can look at a few other deep problems in his Administration now.

Obama's Executive Orders

Obama signed an order to close the terrorists' prison at Guantanamo Bay. As far as we know, the 245 terrorists who are being held there are going to go free, one way or another. Two hundred and forty-five seeds of hatred, murder and death are about to be released into the world. How long will it be until their hatred blooms?

Obama claimed that this was in the interest of human rights. But what about the rights of those humans whose children will be maimed by the bombs these terrorist make once they are released? What about the rights of those humans who will be going to work in the morning, or coming home in the evening somewhere in the world whose last experience on this earth will be the blinding flash of death touched off by one of these madmen?

What about the rights of humans who are enslaved like female cattle under *Sharia* law because these psychopathic seventh-century rejects have been set free? What about those human rights?

And this was the first week of Obama's presidency! If this was the first thing he did as President what worse thing was yet to come?

Actually, we didn't have to wait long. What was worse was that Obama signed another order that prohibited threats, coercion, physical abuse and water-boarding while interrogating detainees. He eliminated the only means we had of getting information from these madmen. He has made criminals of the men who were trying to protect their country. He was trying to play an honorable game with creatures for whom no honor exists. He began his Presidency by doing a dangerous disservice to the country.

At the same time, he forced the CIA to close its secret network of prisons. It was not just the two hundred and forty-five at Gitmo who are going to be unleashed on the world. There are believed to be as many as a hundred prisoners throughout the rest of the world who also will have to be let go.

Obama signed yet another executive order reversing Bush's limits on embryonic stem-cell research. But life begins at conception, when the egg is fertilized by the sperm. Just look at what happens to a tomato. When you plant a tomato seed and a sprout begins to grow, we all understand that there is life there, even though you don't have a whole tomato yet. It is amazing that Obama made this move just when scientists are now developing alternatives to stem-cell research which do not destroy human life. Shouldn't we use these instead of buying into the liberal culture of death?

Obama's flub of the oath of office was not an auspicious beginning to his presidency. His first executive orders were not an auspicious start for the next four years in America or the world.

Yet when conservatives objected to all this, they were castigated in the media for not giving Obama a chance. Supposedly, we were obligated to wait for the duration of a "honeymoon period." But Obama didn't wait. He rushed to pile on his executive orders. How could anyone refuse to analyze them and object to what was wrong in them?

The Obama Cabinet Follies

In addition to his other problems, Obama got involved in a series of appointee scandals. For example, the man Obama appointed as the Federal

Government's chief information officer was raided by the FBI. Vivek Kundra used to be the chief technology officer for Washington D.C. before Obama appointed him, and two men who worked for him were arrested as part of a federal bribery sting. Their names were Yusuf Acar and Sushil Bansal. Kundra had to go on leave from his White House job during the investigation. Authorities said that Kundra's associates defrauded the government by billing for false items and paying non-existent contractors. He was eventually cleared to return to work.

And this was only one in a long list of scandals involving Obama appointees.

- Tim Geithner, Obama's pick for Treasury Secretary "forgot" to pay taxes but was approved anyway. He told transparent lies to justify his story of forgetfulness and no one called him on it.

- Bill Richardson took himself out of the running to be U.S. Commerce Secretary, supposedly because of an on-going investigation into a possible "pay-for-play" deal in Richardson's state.

- Nancy Killefer took herself out of the running for Obama's newly created "chief performance officer" position because she failed for eighteen months to pay employment taxes on household help.

- Tom Daschle forgot to pay $100,000 dollars in taxes and had to step down.

- The husband of Obama's nominee for US labor secretary, Hilda Solis, had more than $7,600 in back taxes still unpaid, but still got approved.

- Ron Kirk, nominated as U.S. trade representative, is the latest of Barack Obama's tax cheaters. He owes an estimated $10,000 in back taxes.

- And the rabid anti-Semite Charles Freeman, Obama's pick for the National Intelligence Council took himself out of the running after his racist comments, as well as his ties to China and Iran, were publicly revealed.

None of these scandals seem to have any effect on Obama's determination to continue appointing corrupt officials. These people think they are above the law. They think the law is for you, the working man, the conservative, the Christian, but not for them.

Is this an administration you can trust to profile conservatives in the name of preventing terrorism?

But it gets worse.

Czar Wars

Back in January 4, 2009, Ranjay Gulati wrote in *Forbes*, "At current growth rates, we are likely to have a car czar, an energy czar, a financial sector czar and a health sector czar."[10] He was not nearly as concerned about this as he should have been. Most of his column is sadly naïve about the nature of all these "strong leaders." But he does at least realize that,

> Almost inevitably, these appointments will go to forceful personal-ities celebrated for their leadership skills. Faced with rescuing entire sectors of our economy, the czars will hire an A-list cadres of aides. Directives will follow; power will gravitate to the positions. And if history is any guide, Washington, instead of fostering solutions, will have added yet another tier of self-protective, self-interested silos to its already impressive landscape.[11]

Gulati is concerned about four of these Czars. At present, Obama has appointed 32 of these people, and he expects to appoint more. In comparison, there were only eighteen Czars in the Romanov family. While all sorts of prob-lems have come to light in Obama's cabinet appointments when they were reviewed by Congress or about to be reviewed, these Czars are never scrutinized by any political authority.

Czars are given amazing powers that the Constitution nowhere empowers the president to give to anyone. They are, as their nickname suggests, offices that are unaccountable and hold great and arbitrary power. They are a means by which a President makes himself a dictator.

Poverty Means Political Power

While Obama gets a free pass in the media to appoint as many unconstitutional "Czars" as he can think of, to appoint as many corrupt-o-crats into his cabinet as he wants, and as he makes a mockery of national security, he is permitted to engage in rank hypocrisy and unprecedented levels of debt-driven spending. As you know, our President shoved a $787 billion stimulus package down the throats of the American people. Apparently it wasn't enough for him. The Democrats then demanded an additional $410 billion of taxpayer money to spend. The spending bill contained 9,000 earmarks–earmarks which Obama promised we wouldn't have. Among the highlights are these:

- $2.2 million for a center for grape genetics in upstate New York.
- $143,000 for Manhattan's American ballet theatre.
- $500,000 for a Senate program to defray the cost of mailing postcards to constituents.
- $200,000 for expenses for a "tattoo removal violence prevention outreach program."
- $5.8 million for the "Ted Kennedy Institute for the Senate."
- $473,000 for National Council of La Raza (as I've said again and again on *Savage Nation, la raza* means "the race" in Spanish, and is a clearly racist organization).

Will Obama admit that he lied about earmarks? Of course not. Did he attempt to justify the way in which he has socialized America so far? Undoubtedly. Did he demand more money for still more socialist programs? Yes.

I have said time and time again on *The Savage Nation* that no one has ever said *no* to Obama. From his childhood through his early career and until now, no authority figure has said, "Stop, you can't do that." So he has developed a sense of self-righteousness and political invincibility.

Now that a weak-kneed Congress has submitted to him on the stimulus bill, he will continue to ask for more and more because it has always worked in the past. And until someone is willing to stand up to him and say, "Stop! Enough! You will not drain the treasury! You will not socialize this country," he will continue to steamroll our freedoms.

Again, as Churchill observed many decades ago, socialism leads to censorship. By taking money away from the people and using it to empower government, Obama is setting up a situation in which speech will be, at best, intimidated. His choice of corrupt cabinet members show very little reason to expect any respect for any aspect of the rule of law.

But we have only just begun looking at what Obama, following Bush, has done to the American economy.

Chapter Notes

[1] "Michael Savage was targeted for being a non-Muslim," July 27, 2009, http://blogs.telegraph.co.uk/news/edwest/100004751/michael-savage-was-targeted-for-being-a-non-muslim/ (Last viewed July 27, 2009).

[2] Ibid.

[3] Associated Press, "G8 Said to Agree on Cuts in Greenhouse Gas Emissions," June 7, 2007, http://www.foxnews.com/story/0,2933,278973,00.html (Last viewed on July 27, 2009).

[4] Peter N. Spotts, "Bush's climate goals vague – but a start," *Christian Science Monitor*, April 18, 2008, http://www.csmonitor.com/2008/0418/p02s01-wogi.htm (Last viewed on July 27, 2009).

[5] Patrick Wintour and Larry Elliott, "Bush under EU pressure to sign up on climate change," *The Guardian*, June 7, 2007, http://www.guardian.co.uk/environment/2007/jun/07/usnews.g8 (Last viewed on July 27, 2009).

[6] Patrick Wintour and Larry Elliott, "Bush signs G8 deal to halve greenhouse gas emissions by 2050," *The Guardian*, June 8, 2007, http://www.guardian.co.uk/world/2008/jul/08/g8 (Last viewed on July 27, 2009).

[7] See Dambisa Moyo's Dead Aid: Why Aid Is Not Working and How There Is a Better Way for Africa (New York: Farrar, Straus and Giroux, 2009).

[8] White House Press Release, "President Bush Attends Briefing on Comprehensive Immigration Reform."

[9] Jeb Bush and Ken Mehlman, "A Good Immigration Bill," *Wall Street Journal*, May 31, 2007, http://online.wsj.com/article/SB118057904673319633.html (Last viewed June 27, 2009).

[10] Ranjay Gulati, "Czar Power," *Forbes*, January 7, 2009, http://www.forbes.com/2009/01/07/obama-appointments-czars-opedcx_rg_0107gulati.html (Last viewed on July 27, 2009).

[11] Ibid.

7

The Financial Takeovers

Back during the Presidential campaign, I observed that the liberal media talking heads were already proclaiming that a Barack Obama victory would be revolutionary–before he even took office. I agreed in a monologue delivered on October 15, 2008, saying, "Revolutionary is right."

The last great revolution took place in Russia. Within a year of the Russian Revolution in 1917, the Communist leader Lenin brought the Russians change they could believe in. He created an economic system in which:

- All industry was nationalized and strict centralized management was introduced.
- Obligatory labor duty was imposed onto "non-working classes" or people who had money.
- Food was rationed and centrally distributed.
- Military-like control of railroads was introduced.
- Private enterprise became illegal.

But that was only the beginning. While people may have thought they were in a total kind of slavery, they actually still had liberty left that, from the perspective of the government, needed to be shut down. So after Stalin took over the Soviet Union, he:

- Imposed a state-run system of socialized medicine
- Formed a strict, centralized cultural administration and an ideological control system–in other words, reeducation.

This last step was the one that Winston Churchill in his wisdom foresaw as a necessary part of any socialist political system. Censorship and the control of speech and writing in all forums are more possible under socialism, in which the government owns all things. And it's more necessary since the government is claiming to be wiser than all its people and their individual decisions. It can't afford for people to be constantly pointing out its many flaws and failures.

So I told my listeners on *The Savage Nation* before Obama came to office that there was every reason to believe that some kind of socialist revolution will occur under Barack Obama. How could anyone expect anything else when supposedly conservative George W. Bush had already imposed socialism on the banks, and Obama promised to do more of the same?

The Soviets put people with money to work in factories. Under Barack Obama, I said, the business owners in this country who drive the economy will be put to work by being forced to pay crushing taxes that will fund gold-plated healthcare for illegal aliens and welfare cases. Private enterprise may not actually be made illegal, but so many businesses will die under an Obama administration that the same goal will be accomplished. I predicted that, instead of trickle-down economics–the liberals' mocking name for Reagan's economic policy–we will have *trickle-up poverty*.

I concluded that we could expect this impoverishment program of socialism to be especially strong in healthcare and censorship:

> We already know Obama will impose socialized medicine. That is a given. And reeducation will come in the form of the Fairness Doctrine, which Nancy Pelosi will push through the Congress by stressing the need to *foster unity* and *avoid destabilizing the markets with hurtful and unbalanced commentary*. This is what the future holds under Barack Obama.

That was from October 15, 2008, on *The Savage Nation*. I told listeners exactly what was going to happen. Now we have some of the frightening details of Obama's Health Care Bill. It would steal from the healthiest and wealthiest Americans in order to pay for gold-plated healthcare for those who refuse to work and for those who are trying to bilk the system.

I have worked hard for forty years to keep myself healthy, and I have worked hard to succeed financially. Why should I be forced to pay for those who have not done so? Of course, to even pose that question to the socialists is to invite ridicule and condemnation. Stealing from those who have, giving to those who have not–just enough for them to survive and vote for you–and lining your pockets with a luxurious cut, is a virtue for them.

People wonder why Nancy Pelosi, possibly the richest woman in Congress, would support a bill that would devastate the economy and spend so much on welfare cases and, in many cases, illegal aliens. But think of the case of Al Gore supporting environmental fascism while he is a partner in a "green" investment firm that needs him to influence politics so they can make money. Or remember Debbie Stabenow who supports the Fairness Doctrine while her husband just happens to be financially invested in Liberal talk radio. I mentioned both of these in Chapter Three.

Pelosi already has her own wealth and she will have plenty of deals she can make from this system to grow it even bigger, and to get even richer. The hit to the economy will prevent most other people from growing wealthy and edging her out of her position of privilege. While it is totally true that economic mobility allows for a society to be wealthier, it is also true that wealthy people all too often prefer a monopoly where they can keep their position and stifle the upward mobility of others.

Which brings us to the greatest change that has occurred in recent days–change that was started not by Barack Obama but by George Bush.

The Bailout Scandals

While most of the mainstream finance media was useless in dealing honestly with what was happening, in 2007 and 2008 the economy started to worsen. There were plenty of issues that caused some people to ask anxious questions, but our leaders assured us that everything was fine, or that there would only be a temporary slowing, until suddenly, on September 18, 2008, Henry Paulson, the Secretary of the Treasury Department, suddenly demanded $750 billion in unaccountable money to use at his discretion to bail out the banks. This was an amazing turn-around, and no one of any importance in the government or the media did anything to hold him responsible. Both he and Federal Reserve Chairman Ben Bernanke had been telling a very different story.

October 27, 2005
Ben Bernanke: A two-year spike in housing prices is not a bubble but "largely reflects strong economic fundamentals."[1]

March 1, 2007
Henry Paulson: "I am watching developments carefully, and believe that the U.S. economy is healthy."[2]

Ben Bernanke: "We are looking for moderate growth in the economy going forward," and markets are "working well."[3]

September 20, 2007
Henry Paulson: "US economic fundamentals are healthy: unemployment is low, wages are rising and core inflation is contained." "Although the recent reappraisal of risk, coupled with weakness in the housing sector, may well result in a penalty, the fundamentals point to continued US economic growth."[4]

November 8, 2007
Ben Bernanke: "We have not calculated the probability of a recession. Our assessment is for slower growth, but positive."[5]

February 15, 2008
Ben Bernanke: The Administration's economic forecast "would be less, but I do believe we'll keep growing."[6]

Of course, it was all delusional. Neither Bernanke nor Paulson admitted that the economy was in trouble until far too late. In fact, that first statement by Bernanke on October 27, 2005, that there was no housing bubble was made when he had just been nominated to replace Alan Greenspan as the Federal Reserve Chairman. He undoubtedly got picked by Bush precisely because Bush wanted someone to tell him everything was wonderful.

In fact, while many economists and financial experts knew that there was a housing bubble, Bernanke said that housing prices skyrocketing out of sight were based on "strong growth in jobs, incomes and the number of new households."[7] This was a reversal of the truth. The reason for growth in jobs, incomes, and new households was due to the housing bubble. Once housing collapsed, a large part of the economy that had become dependent upon it was heavily damaged–and still is.

Bush did not want to admit that the economy was weakening under his regime. He made us believe we could go on spending and running up credit cards while the United States fought to control and stabilize at least two countries. Cracks began to surface but they were constantly fixed by government action with ridiculous assurances that the economy had now been saved.

What happened? First and foremost, Bush did not want economic recession or even slower growth during his presidency. From May 16, 2000 to June 21, 2003, the Federal Funds Rate–the interest rate that banks have to pay the Federal Reserve on loans–went from 6.5 % to 1%. Most of that lowering happened in 2001–a year that saw eleven cuts in the rate–dramatically more decreases in interest than had ever been tried before.[8] This discouraged savings since it undercut the reward for savings, especially with inflation, and it encouraged borrowing.

In 2002 and following, the need to find ways to make a profit with an easy money environment that discouraged savings found a target in the housing market. Investors wanted a place to park their money and the government was encouraging more home ownership for those who ordinarily would not be able to afford a mortgage. Low interest rates were already encouraging institutions to extend credit. Fannie Mae and Freddie Mac helped since, "The Department of Housing and Urban Development allowed housing finance institutions Fannie Mae and Freddie Mac to count billions of dollars they purchased in subprime securities as fulfilling their government mandate to help make buying a home more affordable."[9]

This bubble got more people into homes by making credit more readily available even while it upped the price of almost all homes and made them all less affordable. Potential home-buyers were all told that the debt was worth it because they could always be sure that they would be able to sell their homes at a higher price. The alleged rising value of homes was used as an excuse not to worry about the fact that the nation's rate of savings was going into the toilet.

Just to be clear, lower income minorities were not helped by being sold these homes. They ended up with adjustable rate mortgages they soon could not afford.[10] It became extremely obvious that "helping" poor minorities became a way for Wall Street to rip them off and make a killing.

Worse, banks and real estate agents began to target illegal immigrants. I don't mean that illegal immigrants fooled real estate agents and banks. I don't even mean that banks got sneaky and secretly began giving loans to illegals. I mean they openly claimed that they should and would extend credit to illegal aliens. Here is a lead paragraph in a story from CNN:

> Despite heated political debate in Washington over illegal immigration in the United States, an increasing number of banks are seeing an untapped resource for growing their own revenue stream and contend that providing undocumented residents with mortgages will help revitalize local communities. It's a win-win situation, they say.[11]

But it was win-lose for the American economy, for the US taxpayer, and probably even for the illegal alien. It was pure exploitation and had nothing to do with real compassion.

In 2004, investment firms got the SEC to waive their normal rules that prohibited them from borrowing at a ratio higher than twelve-to-one. Five firms, and only five firms, were given this special exemption from the rule: *Goldman Sachs, Merrill Lynch, Lehman Brothers, Bear Stearns* and *Morgan Stanley*. These firms loaded up on debt to use in the stock market. Their debt-to-asset ratio was sometimes admitted to be as high as forty-to-one.[12] These firms were playing with fire, but most of them would use the same power that got the rule about too much debt canceled to also pass on the consequences to the American taxpayer.

A hint of foretaste of what was to come was given to us in June 2008 when Christopher Dodd announced a bill that would use a new Federal Housing Administration refinancing program to give mortgage lenders a way to make taxpayers take care of up to $300 billion of their worst loans.[13] He shamelessly made this announcement the same day that he admitted that he got "special" treatment from Countrywide.[14] Countrywide stood to benefit by up to $25 billion from his proposal, yet Dodd said that even though he knew he was a special customer, he did not know he was getting a special deal when Countrywide gave him a $75,000 reduction in his mortgage payment.[15]

Dodd's claim to be innocent of corruption is shameless and unbelievable. He is a powerful Senator who is also the head of the Senate Banking Committee. Senator Kent Conrad got similar special favors from Countrywide. He too claims to have been blissfully unaware of the favors he was getting. Conrad is the chairman of the Senate Budget Committee.

The Countrywide official has testified to Congress that the Senators were told that they were getting special favors.[16] If by some chance this particular scandal is not proven true, the fact remains that between lobbying money and many other deal-making opportunities, these bailouts are inherently corrupt.

Economic bad news piled up until suddenly, on September 18, 2008, Henry Paulson said he needed $700 billion to spend as he saw fit to take care of "toxic assets"–mortgage-backed securities that were essentially worthless. This was a tax on the working middle-class to bail out the rich Wall Street bankers and investment managers.

Bush claimed that, "I've abandoned free-market principles to save the free-market system," and said he acted because, "I feel a sense of obligation to my successor to make sure there is not a, you know, a huge economic crisis." This was widely reported and you can find it all over the internet, but to get the full effect of the hypocrisy, I recommend viewing the actual footage from the CNN interview on YouTube.[17] It is stunning to watch.

What garbage! Did Bush feel the need to abandon "free-market principles" when he was supporting NAFTA or other free-trade follies? Did he ever allow us to believe that it was right to compromise his beloved "free-market principles" when he was out there advocating amnesty for illegal aliens and lobbying for a guest worker program?

The truth is that Bush's true loyalties have always been to his wealthy friends and supporters who benefited from cheap labor and investment overseas. Now, suddenly, those friends were in financial danger and following "free-market principles" was no longer convenient for them. So he immediately implemented socialism. He never compromised his true beliefs because his true belief was always in his own ruling class and its inherent right to always be on top of the nation. Whether that meant ignoring our immigration laws or stealing from the nation's economy to directly subsidize his friends, Bush always did what was necessary to protect his core belief in his own class.

What America has learned from the 2008 presidential race was that Obama is the socialist leader of the poor. Again and again he expressed his desire to give the poor free healthcare, free drugs, and free housing. His base is the welfare class who wants to take what they can from those that produce real wealth in this society. And, so naturally, his programs will be paid for by tax increases on working Americans–despite his deceitful denials during the campaign season.

But where did President George Bush stand? He was opposed to a welfare state for the nation's poor, but bailouts for billionaires were just fine. Bush was the socialist leader of the rich. He was fine with welfare for the wealthy. And he, too, was willing to tax working Americans. But instead of giving the money to the homeless and the welfare cases, he gave it to the rich so they could buy another jet, or a third house in the Hamptons.

So we have Obama as the socialist leader of the poor. We had Bush as the socialist leader of the rich. And we had John McCain as the clueless leader of the illegals. We had no serious candidate who was not going to try to screw working American citizens out of their paychecks. There is no hope in looking to the leaders in either major political parties; look to the people of a more *Savage Nation*.

Bailout Mania

What is amazing about the first bailout–dubbed TARP for Troubled Asset Relief Program–was that the American people *rejected* it, despite an incredible and completely deceptive campaign by the major media, and the cooperation of many so-called "conservative" blogs, news outlets, economists, and think-tanks.

They not only did so in surveys and in phone calls to Congress, but also legally through their representatives in Congress. They made it known, clearly and emphatically, that they did not want to give a cent to Wall Street.

Yet the self-styled "maverick" John McCain, and Barack Obama, who spoke against "politics as usual" in the name of fiscal responsibility, *both* shamelessly supported the bailout and simply ignored the will of the people. Of course, I know that we aren't ruled by "direct democracy." But when the law in question fundamentally changes the nature of the American government and economy, popular opinion should carry a great deal of weight. How dare these candidates pretend to care about America and yet shove down their throats their preference for empowering the Department of the Treasury with virtually three quarter of a trillion dollars and no accountability on how it's spent?

But they did, and the media never even questioned them about it. *How could this have happened?*

To answer the question, all you needed to do is look at their top campaign contributors. Citigroup gave almost $300,000 to McCain and over $450,000 to Obama. JP Morgan gave about a half-million to Obama and about $200,000 to McCain. Goldman Sachs, Hank Paulson's old company, gave a quarter-million to McCain and three-quarters of a million to Obama.

Citigroup. JP Morgan. Goldman Sachs. These are the very companies that McCain and Obama helped give a trillion dollars to. The candidates never answered to the people. They answered to the powerful.

On the media stage, Obama and McCain appeared to be separate actors. But if you pulled back the curtain, you would find that they were merely puppets on different hands of the same powerful oligarchy. Their movements are contrived to make you believe that there is an actual choice between candidates with different positions. But the receipts tell a different story.

The situation nearly reached the point of comedy the day after Congress—in obedience to the will of the people—voted TARP down. The oligarchy through Paulson and the media had predicted Armageddon if the bailout didn't happen quickly. The day after it was voted down, Armageddon didn't come. Instead, the Dow went up almost 500 points. The markets actually went up without the bailout. But on that same day, Bush and Obama and Paulson and McCain spoke with one voice. They still wanted the bailout. McCain said they would bail out Wall Street whether you wanted it or not. The truth was so obvious to everyone, even as the media totally ignored it. The bailout is not designed to help the economy; rather the bailout is designed to help the oligarchy.

The agents of the oligarchy were enraged when they heard the voice of the people say that they would not give Wall Street another penny. Republican hacks decried populism. Democrat leftists raged that the people would not go along with their plan for socializing the economy. The oligarch-in-chief, George W. Bush, came out and said, "It matters little what path a bill takes to become law. What matters is that we get a law."

And, John McCain, the great conservative, said that "The Treasury has at its disposal about a trillion dollars that they could begin, without congressional authority, buying up some of these terrible mortgages and help stabilize the situation." So McCain says screw the people, we'll bail out Wall Street anyway. Without the approval of Congress. Without the approval of the people. This is the oligarchy in its most naked, insidious form.

The oligarchy showed it will do anything it takes, to get what it wants. It will try to scare you by saying you won't be able to get a car loan. It will try to threaten you by saying that the markets will crash if it doesn't get its way. But if you still say no, they will say, "Screw you, we're doing it anyway. We know better than you. We'll do what we want to."

Later, once Obama was in the Oval Office, a new "scandal" erupted. Barak Obama claimed to be outraged over the fact that AIG, which has received tens of billions of taxpayer dollars to keep it afloat, had given $160 million worth of retention bonuses to its executives and other employees. He was so outraged that Obama even claimed to have gotten choked up over it at a press conference.

But it turns out that his outrage was possibly nothing more than simply crocodile tears. According to the records, Obama received a total of over $100,000 worth of campaign contributions from AIG during the 2008 election cycle—a nice little bonus of his own. So Obama may be talking big, but as I said on *The Savage Nation*, "in the end we'll see what actually gets done to take the money back from these thieves."

What about Timothy Geithner, the boy Treasury Secretary? He is supposed to be in charge of getting this money back. That's an interesting story too, because, as it happens, he played a pivotal role in bailing out AIG to begin with.

Even when Congress was supposed to be grilling AIG CEO Edward Liddy on Capitol Hill, it seemed like one congressman after another made a point of saying he wasn't to blame—one excuse after another. Perhaps Obama isn't the only one that AIG has given money to. Even leftists protesters who were at the hearing, and who for once I agreed with, were told by the Chairman Representative

Kanjorski to put down their signs, some of which said, "Fire Geithner." It seems that not even the Marxist wing of the Democratic Party has been able to overcome all the money that has been spread around Washington D.C. by AIG.

Looks like when it comes to the Democrats, being left is good, but having loot is better.

Gangster Government

When TARP was forced through Congress a second time so that it passed, the premise was that the money would be used to buy up toxic assets. But Henry Paulson was making things up as he went along and really had no idea what to do about the economy. He just wanted a lot of money to experiment with. By the time he actually got the authorization, his plans had changed and he decided that what was needed was for the Treasury Department to get a controlling interest in the banks.

To give a strong start to his plan, Paulson summoned the CEOs of the nine largest banks to meet with him at a conference room in the Treasury Department on Monday, October 13, 2008. There, they were surprised to be seated at a table in alphabetical order across from Paulson, Bernanke, Tim Geithner—who was then the Chairman of the New York Federal Reserve and probably already assured to be Paulson's successor in the Obama Administration—and Sheila Bair, the chief of the FDIC.[18] They were each handed a single-page document that agreed to sell shares to the government, and were told they were not leaving until they signed it.

The main holdout was the chairman of Wells Fargo, Richard Kovacevich, who did not want or need any money from the Federal Government. Nevertheless, he signed the agreement by 6:30 pm like all the other CEOs. According to the *New York Times*, "What happened during those three and a half hours is a story of high drama and brief conflict, followed by acquiescence by the bankers, who felt they had little choice but to go along with the Treasury plan to inject $250 billion of capital into thousands of banks, starting with theirs."[19]

Deborah Solomon, who broke the story, gave this answer to the question of how Paulson convinced them all to do it:

He basically said it's the collective good, but he drove a hard bargain. He sort of–we've been joking it was sort of his mafia moment. He made them an offer they couldn't refuse. Dick Kovacevich, who is the head of Wells Fargo, basically was arguing–and probably rightly so–we don't need more capital. You know, we are basically going to raise capital because we're taking over Wachovia. We don't want to have too much capital. We don't think we need to be a part of this program. And Mr. Paulson put it in pretty blunt terms. He said, look, you can turn us down now, but if it turns out that you need to go out and raise more money–you know, we don't know what's going to happen. You may at some point need more capital. If that happens and you go out and you can't find a private investor to give you money, God help you if you come back to me, because you're not going to get as good terms and conditions the second time around. This is your shot.

Solomon can say that "a mafia moment" is a joke, but she is wrong. She knows full well and has told us that a powerful office holder in the Federal Government used his position to force a bank CEO to give him ownership. If we were not a corrupt banana republic already, we became one the moment this event became widely known and the authorities and media shrugged it off as something to joke about.

It later turned out that Paulson and Bernanke had already had a chance to practice their gangsterism. Back on September 16, one of the many financial deals cobbled together to protect the economy was Bank of America's acquisition of Merrill Lynch. The $50 billion deal was completed so fast that everyone was sure that the Federal Reserve must have pressured it, but the CEO of Bank of America, Ken Lewis, denied this.

"There was no pressure from regulators, absolutely no pressure," said Mr. Lewis, who described the deal as "the strategic opportunity of a lifetime." He said: "The first contact came on Saturday morning and we put the transaction together in 48 hours. The instant we talked it made sense."[20]

But this was not true. There was a great deal of pressure. Furthermore, by December 14, Lewis was made aware of further billions of dollars of losses that Merrill Lynch had suffered. Consulting with a lawyer, Lewis found he had the ability and obligation to halt the merger on the grounds of a Material Adverse Conditions (MAC) clause in the contract. But when he told Paulson he was considering invoking the MAC clause to get out of the deal, Paulson told him that he would replace Bank of America's board if he did so. Paulson and Bernanke also directed him not to disclose Merrill Lynch's losses.[21] According to the Attorney General to the state of New York, Andrew Cuomo:

> Notably, during Bank of America's important communications with federal banking officials in late December 2008, the lone federal agency charged with protecting investor interests, the Securities and Exchange Commission, appears to have been kept in the dark. Indeed, Secretary Paulson informed this Office that he did not keep the SEC Chairman in the loop during the discussions and negotiations with Bank of America in December 2008.[22]

Of course, the SEC had to be kept in the dark since Paulson and Bernanke were coercing the CEO of Bank of America to do things that were detrimental to stockholders.

Why am I telling you all this in a book that is mostly about free speech? The point here is that well before Obama took office, and even before the election, the United States was already being run like a gangster kingdom. People were being pressured and threatened.

It is important that you realize that we are being run like a banana republic. It is important because the MIAC strategic report and the Department of Homeland Security's "Rightwing Extremism" report are coming out of a government run by people who do not hesitate to threaten and lie to get their way, who do not care about the rule of law, and who have the power to intimidate and perhaps even censor.

This started under Bush, and it is just as bad under Obama.

Obama, in addition to passing more extraordinarily expensive spending (misnamed "stimulus"), and bailing out AIG again and putting more money into

TARP, has also taken over much of the car industry in the United States. And how was that done?

> Creditors to Chrysler describe negotiations with the company and the Obama administration as "a farce," saying the administration was bent on forcing their hands using hardball tactics and threats. Conversations with administration officials left them expecting that they would be politically targeted, two participants in the negotiations said. Although the focus has so far been on allegations that the White House threatened Perella Weinberg, sources familiar with the matter say that other firms felt they were threatened as well. None of the sources would agree to speak except on the condition of anonymity, citing fear of political repercussions.[23]

These people claimed to have actually voted for Obama in the election, but now "they were taken aback by the hardball tactics" that his administration employed. One witness said that "the administration's tactic was to present what one described as a 'madman theory of the presidency'" and that they should fear Obama because he "was willing to do anything to get his way." He said that his firm took the threat "very seriously."[24]

As one would expect, the White House denies threatening and intimidating. But how can we take such denials seriously? The way Obama treated free speech while he was on the campaign trail was atrocious. His "truth squad" should raise all kinds of questions about his character. And, to make matters worse, Bush appointee Henry Paulson showed the same sort of behavior, forcing people to do what he wanted and telling them what message they must give to the public. This is all about power and control–a power and control that both has the ability to censor or intimidate speech as well as a need to do so in order to prevent people from objecting to what the government is doing.

Socialism Just Means Gangsterism

Now that the Bank of America has the majority of its shares owned by the government, the United States of America stands at a perilous crossroads. The largest bank in America is now government-owned, and we are careening towards what the media refers to as nationalization. What it is, in fact, is a socialization of the banks—a communizing of the entire financial system of the country. George W. Bush pushed us most of the way towards this leftist end. And then Citigroup was socialized as well. They were the largest contributor to Obama's inauguration party. Considering how the government took over General Motors, it looks like we're moving towards complete communism.

How did we get to this point? The truth is that those who proclaimed themselves to be capitalists were never really capitalists. They were only hucksters and gangsters. They claimed to be for free enterprise, but all they wanted was more money by whatever means necessary. In this case, it was by direct theft from the American people. So when their own greed and stupidity caught up with them, they came running to the government for a bailout, abandoning principles for avarice. And what elite group will we be joining if we continue down the path to socialize companies? England, France, and Venezuela. They've all gone the same way. The old cold warriors can rail against communism all they like. But the bankers have suddenly realized that communism can be profitable, too. It's just a different way of screwing the people.

In the former Soviet Union, *Pravda* was the official newspaper and it always printed all the news the government decided was fit to print. Already, a company that owns a major news outlet expects big bucks from the government. General Electric, which owns MSNBC, stands to make a fortune from the Obama Administration's "green" agenda.[25] Politicians are openly calling for a bailout of the press.[26] We may have our own *Pravda* sooner than you think.

With socialization of companies and censorship and propaganda, our transformation to a communist country will be complete.

Chapter Notes

[1] Nell Henderson, "Bernanke: There's No Housing Bubble to Go Bust," *Washington Post*, October 27, 2005; Page D01 http://www.washingtonpost. com/wpdyn/content/article/2005/10/26/AR2005102602255.html (Last viewed on July 28, 2009).

[2] Steve Matthews and Scott Lanman, "Bernanke, Learning From Mistakes, Reassures Markets," *Bloomberg News*, March 1, 2007, http://www.bloomberg. com /apps/news?pid=20601109&sid=aU7mMzddpKwQ (Viewed July 28, 2009).

[3] Nell Henderson and David Cho, "Markets 'Working Well,' Says Fed Chief," *Washington Post*, Thursday, March 1, 2007; Page A01 http://www.washingtonpost.com/wp-dyn/content/article/2007/02/28/ AR2007022802116.html (Last viewed on July 28, 2009).

[4] "Paulson again downplays credit crisis, expects continued economic growth," *Forbes*, September 20, 2007, http://www.forbes.com/feeds/ afx/2007/09/20/afx4139316.html (Last viewed on July 28, 2009).

[5] Edmund L. Andrews, "Fed chief warns of worse times in the economy," *New York Times*, November 8, 2007, http://www.nytimes.com/ 2007/11/09/busi-ness/worldbusiness/09iht-09fed.8260152.html (Last viewed on July 28, 2009).

[6] Edmund L. Andrews, "Bernanke and Paulson criticized over their response to U.S. economic woes," February 15, 2008, http://www.nytimes. com/2008/ 02/15/business/worldbusiness/15iht-usecon.1.10075792.html (Last viewed on July 28, 2009).

[7] Nell Henderson, Ibid.

[8] Information provided at the Federal Reserve's website, http://www. federalreserve.gov/fomc/fundsrate.htm

[9] "Buying Subprime Securities," *Washington Post*, June 10, 2008, http://www.washingtonpost.com/wp-dyn/content/graphic/2008/06/10/ GR2008061000059.html (Last viewed July 10, 2008).

[10] Sue Kirchhoff and Judy Keen, "Minorities hit hard by rising costs of subprime loans," *USA Today*, April 25, 2007, http://www.usatoday.com/money/economy/housing/2007-04-25-subprime-minorities-usat_N.htm (Last viewed July 28, 2007).

[11] Shaheen Pasha, "Banking on illegal immigrants," *CNN Money*, August 8, 2005. http://money.cnn.com/2005/08/08/news/economy/illegal_immigrants/ (Last viewed on July 28, 2009).

[12] Barry L. Ritholtz, "A Memo Found in the Street: Uncle Sam the Enabler," *Barron's*, September 29, 2008, http://online.barrons.com/article/SB122246742997580395.html, (Last viewed on July 28, 2009).

[13] "Angelo's Angel," *Wall Street Journal*, June 19, 2008, http://online.wsj.com/article/SB121383295591086669.html (Last viewed on July 28, 2009).

[14] Ibid.

[15] Ibid.

[16] Larry Margasak, "AP IMPACT: Dodd, Conrad told deals were sweetened," Associated Press.

[17] I found it at http://www.youtube.com/watch?v=oetNPJJcuAE (Last viewed on July 28, 2009).

[18] These details of the story are found in an interview with Deborah Solomon who broke the story in the *Wall Street Journal*. The interview, "Anatomy of a Financial Bailout," was conducted by NPR's *All Things Considered*. Both audio and transcript can be found at http://www.npr.org/templates/story/story.php?storyId=95748764

[19] Mark Landler and Eric Dash, "Drama–and conflict–behind the $250 billion banking deal," *New York Times*, October 15, 2008. http://www.nytimes.com/2008/10/15/business/worldbusiness/15iht-bailout.4.16986910.html (Last viewed July 28, 2009).

[20] Carl Mortished, "Bank of America emerges from the frenzy with Merrill Lynch to lead 'thundering herd,'" *The Times*, September 16, 2008.

[21] "Text of Cuomo letter on Merrill Lynch takeover," *MarketWatch*, April 23, 2009.

[22] Ibid.

[23] John Carney, "New Allegations Of White House Threats Over Chrysler," *The Business Insider*, May 5, 2009, http://www.businessinsider.com /new-allegations-of-white-house-threats-over-chysler-2009-5 (Last viewed July 28, 2009).

[24] Ibid.

[25] Timothy P. Carney, "Obama's hidden bailout of General Electric," *Washington Examiner*, March 4, 2009, http://www.washingtonexaminer.com/ politics/Obamas-hidden-bailout-of-General-Electric_03_04-40686707.html (Last viewed July 28, 2009).

[26] Robert MacMillan, "Government aid could save U.S. newspapers, spark debate," *Reuters*, Dec 31, 2008, http://www.reuters.com/article/reutersEdge/ idUSTRE4BU53T20081231 (Last viewed on July 28, 2009).

8

The Fight Goes On

Where do we go from here?

Of course, I have to answer that question for myself. Much of this book is the story of my own fight for free speech. Obviously, *I* have to keep doing what I am doing. I have to keep fighting in the courts for vindication. I have to keep using my lawyers to get information involved in the decision against me. There may be more secret communications the bureaucrats want to hide. I have to keep raising money for my defense fund. I also have to keep telling the truth about myself and who I am. I have to disprove the vicious fake version of me banned by the British government.

But this is not only about me. I have the odd and unique privilege to represent two important groups in America. I represent the battle for the freedom of conservative talk radio, and conservatives across the nation. I also represent the right of any true independent to be left alone; to be uncensored and uncoerced in modern society.

In both cases, in America, speech is not supposed to be intimidated or censored. What has happened to me slips through the cracks because it was done by the British Home Office. But it was done by a strong ally who had to have some sort of support from someone, or some agency, in the United States. As I have pointed out, there is no other likely way that the Home Office would have ever heard of me. I have yet to find out to what extent the American help consisted of–private citizens or public politicians–or the murky ground in between.

At the same time we have a government at home that is openly intimidating political speech through Homeland Security and aggrandizing power over businesses through bailouts and bullying. We have the constant specter of the so-called "Fairness Doctrine" aimed at destroying Talk Radio. We have the media being offered bailouts so that it becomes in fact what it already effectively is in practice–the state media. We have the possibility of Hate Crimes legislation and other things that could officially end real free speech.

We also have a host of national security issues abroad that need real solutions rather than hope and posturing. Islamofascism and Hispanocommunism in South America–and North Korea and China–all require strong leadership that we don't have.

We independent conservatives may feel overwhelmed, but we need to keep standing up for what is right.

As I pointed out in Chapter 6, it isn't realistic to separate domestic policy and civil liberties from foreign policy and national security. Refusal to acknowledge the dire threat that is Islamofascism means one is forced to engage in all sorts of cover-ups and censorships. This is happening internationally. When my banning from Britain was covered in Canada's *Jewish Tribune*, the writer pointed out there is an international context for what happened in the United Nations. "In March 2009, the United Nations Human Rights Council passed Resolution A/HRC/10/L calling for the 'creation of laws in member states to prevent criticism of religions' (Islam)."[1]

The UN's anti-blasphemy resolution was written by Pakistan and presented by the Organization of the Islamic Conference. The UN Council, with a vote of 23 countries supporting the measure, 11 opposed and 13 abstaining, passed it in March 2009. The resolution states, in part, the following:

- Defamation of religions is a serious affront to human dignity;
- The need to effectively combat defamation of all religions and incitement to religious hatred in general and against Islam and Muslims in particular;
- Islam is frequently and wrongly associated with human rights violations and terrorism; and
- Urges all states to provide, within their respective legal and constitutional systems, adequate protection against acts of hatred, discrimination, intimidation and coercion resulting from defamation of religions and incitement to religious hatred in general.[2]

This resolution is completely contradictory to the United Nations' own Declaration of Human Rights. Sadly, this contradiction is appearing in many Western nations, where liberals seem unable to deal with Islamic pressure. Free speech and other aspects of the rule of law are being reduced. The commitment that government is supposed to have toward national security and impartial justice become questionable. This is done in response to pressure from countries where non-Islam religions are regularly persecuted and are, at the very least, not adequately protected by their governments from local extremist violence. What is worse, once this happens enough to make one question the authorities, it becomes impossible to trust them to do their job.

When the story hit locally in San Francisco, I was the only one in national media to talk about the death of Dr. Daniel J. Kliman.[3] He was a pro-Israel activist Jew who was mysteriously found at the bottom of an elevator shaft in the same building where he had been taking Arabic classes for three years. I was the only one in the national or local media to tell Savage listeners that this looked like foul play. And I was the only one who had the inspector in charge of the case on his show to ask the key questions that needed to be asked.

I refused to let the story die.

Soon there were more questions. I reported on *The Savage Nation* that prior to his death, Kliman was at a pro-Israel event at the University of California at Berkeley where violence erupted with a group called Students for Justice in Palestine. Kliman had called on pro-Israel activists in the community to bring Israeli flags and stand with Zionist students at Berkeley for a vigil. Mysteriously, he was found dead at the bottom of an elevator shaft two weeks later.

I also was informed that there appeared to be signs of a struggle on the outside of the elevator doors on the same floor in the building where Kliman met his death. I learned this, not thanks to the efforts of the San Francisco Police Department, but because of an individual who had the brains to go to the building, take pictures, and post them on his website. If there was a struggle outside of the elevator on the seventh floor where we know Kliman went, then this would seem to obliterate the police theory that his death was an accident which occurred as he was trying to escape from the inside of a broken elevator.

As the tale became more and more curious, the San Francisco Police

Department didn't seem to be very curious. Remember the old movies where the policeman would say "move along people, nothing to see here?" That's what the San Francisco police department has been trying to say. In fact, when my staff called the inspector we had interviewed on the show the day before, he said the department had prohibited him from talking to us.

The San Francisco Police Department treated all questions about the death, and all suspicions that it was not an accident, as a "conspiracy" theory. I have no way of really knowing how they arrived at their decision that Kliman's death was an accident. Many of their claims about how it must have happened appeared to be guesswork. And they made statements about the elevator doors that seemed to be contradicted by other testimony and the elevator's own inspection records.

Of course, I can't prove anything for certain. Maybe it was some sort of amazing accident. But that's unlikely. However, it does serve as an example of how the fear of offending an ethnic group in our midst is poisoning the public trust.

It's too easy to multiply examples of this problem of refusing to acknowledge or trying to cover for the threat of Islamic extremists. When an 82-year-old anti-Semite attacked the holocaust museum, it was pinned on conservatives and used to defend the ridiculous Homeland Security reports that had come out. But when Abdulhakim Mujahid Muhammad opened fire at a recruiting station, killing a U.S. soldier and wounding another, we never heard anything about the danger we face from domestic Islamic terrorism. Blasting conservatives is completely acceptable in the media and in the Administration, even when the person involved is not a conservative. But Islamofascists get a pass.

The problem is not simply government or the news media. When Hitler came to power in the 1930s, his propaganda minister Joseph Goebbels began to purge the German culture of Jews and others who were politically or artistically suspect. On May 10, 1933, university students burned upwards of 25,000 volumes of "un-German" books. That night, students marched in torchlight parades "against the un-German spirit."

A generation ago, Ayatollah Khomeini of Iran, another Middle Eastern Hitler, ordered the death of Salman Rushdie, the author of *The Satanic Verses,* for blasphemous references against Islam. Even though he's been dead for years, the order has never been rescinded.

Today, Islamofascists aren't burning books, or even ordering the death of their authors. They're stopping them before they're even printed. Sherry Jones wrote a novel about Mohammed's wife called *The Jewell of Medina* that was to be published by Random House. But after consulting Islamic scholars, Random House decided that the book might be offensive to some in the Muslim community, so they decided not to publish it.

What's worse is that the person behind this blatant censorship is not a Muslim cleric, but a far left professor of Islamic history, Denise Spellberg. She started the push to get the book dumped and threatened to sue the publisher. And now the book has been more effectively destroyed than it could have been in a Nazi bonfire.

Let me say it again: free speech is being destroyed, not just in America, but globally. Ideas are being crushed because they are offensive to the State. Ideas are being cleansed from our culture to make it safe and pure. And just as under Hitler's Germany, it is the Kapos, the condemned themselves, who are opening the door to the ovens.

And of course, our foreign policy needs to be realistic, not based on fantasy.

In the midst of its adulation of Barak Hussein Obama, the liberal American media seems to have forgotten that there is a dire threat to western civilization in the form of Islamofascist terrorism. Not too long ago the media was full of favorable coverage of Hillary Clinton reaching out to the Muslims and trying to eliminate prejudice against them in the United States. That is the wrong focus. Clinton's focus must be to work with other countries to *defeat* Muslim terrorists across the world.

Terrorism has not suddenly come to an end simply because the media decides not to cover it. British Muslims were recently caught in a plot to destroy airplanes with soda cans. A Muslim group in Australia called on Muslims to start forest fires as a form of jihad. And the world already seems to have forgotten the hundreds that were killed in Bombay, India as a result of their terrorism.

The liberal media doesn't want you to remember these things. Is it because the only response to a threat that a liberal can imagine is to cower and capitulate? Is it because powerful Saudi investors have a large financial stake in media companies such as News Corp, Rupert Murdoch's liberal media empire that includes the "conservative" Fox News? Who knows? But Hillary Clinton has offered a carrot where we need a stick. Hillary Clinton may be Secretary of State, but that won't matter much if we have no state. If we place ourselves at the mercy of madmen, and open the gates of our civilization to an army of fanatics, then we have lost. And there is no guarantee that we will win. History teaches us that Rome was eventually conquered by the barbarians. We have become as soft as Rome, we have become as degenerate as Rome, and we have become as corrupt as Rome. Rome fell, England is falling, and it seems like we may be next on the list.

To face this challenge will require bold leadership. Real leadership.

"Dulce et decorum est pro patria mori" is a line from the Roman poet Horace. In English, it means, "It is sweet and honorable to die for one's country."

And it's true.

Many brave men died so this country could be born in the Revolutionary War. Many men died to keep it from being destroyed by secession in the Civil War. And many died to keep the specter of fascism from conquering the globe in World War Two.

But when the voices for war are neoconservative hacks, the words lose their power. When old men from inside the Washington beltway beat the drums for a war with Iran they would not enter themselves, it becomes meaningless. When the call for action comes from those who are themselves action*less*, the words turn sour. America will not stand for a war run by old men with prostate problems who have no idea how to do it. America will not go to battle when they are led from behind.

America longs for the day when a brave man or woman, a real leader, will stand up and say, "We must crush the enemy before we ourselves are crushed. Let me be the first on the front lines." But if we depend on the beltway bozos, if we rely on the neo-conservative ninnies, and if we count on the Georgetown gigolos, we will be sorely disappointed.

Theodore Roosevelt volunteered for the front lines of World War One. Winston Churchill resigned from government to fight on the Western Front. FDR's sons fought in World War Two in the Navy, Air Force, and Marine Corps. Where are those kind of brave men today? Where are those for whom a war means the possibility of real loss, of real danger?

"Dulce et decorum est pro patria mori." It is sweet and honorable to die for one's country. Some things are worth dying for, but words will fail if they do not come with action.

Toothless in North Korea

It was an all too rare moment of glory when the United States of America triumphed over the pirates. The Muslim malcontents had a machine gun leveled at the captured captain's back on their boat and U.S. navy snipers killed them with a single bullet each. Captain Richard Phillips was freed five days after his ship was hijacked off the Somali coast.

The real credit here goes to the Navy Seals who shot these pirates. They performed their duties superbly and gave honor to their country's name. And we should also salute Obama for his resolve in ending the pirate takeover of the cargo vessel and the killing of the pirates.

However, if we ask the question, "Has Obama faced his first military challenge and won?" The answer is: *Absolutely not.* This was not a real military challenge. It was a piracy challenge. Obama's first military challenge was from North Korea. Kim Jong *mentally*-Ill fired a rocket. Obama failed to stop him from doing so, and failed to act in any meaningful way. That cannot be forgotten no matter how glad we are that he acted against the pirates.

The latest fiasco when the North Korean regime kidnapped (oh, am I supposed to say "imprisoned"?) two journalists for wanting to get a story about how the government is inflicting its people with horrible poverty is another example. Did sending Bill Clinton to beg for mercy really show the world that we are a superpower who wants to defend civilization? Why didn't we just start paying off the pirates if that is our attitude?

Truthfully, the Bush Administration did not do any better. All this talk about the axis of evil, after all, is only talk.

In 2006, the stammering schoolmarm, Condoleezza Rice, came on television to say that North Korea would pay a price for their nuclear test in the form of United Nations sanctions. Give sanctions more time, she said. But anyone who examined the so-called sanctions the UN imposed on North Korea would know they couldn't work.

Look at these sanctions:

One: Ban the sale to, or export from, North Korea of military hardware. *Too late.*

Two: Ban the sale or export of nuclear and missile related items. *Again, too late.*

Three: Ban the sale of luxury goods. *Insane. Half of North Korea is eating shoe leather and the UN wants to cut off all sales of caviar.*

Four: Freeze finances and ban travel. *Again, this is insanity. There are no finances to freeze and the only people to suffer from a travel ban would be Sandy Berger and Madeline Albright.*

Five: Allow inspection of cargo to and from North Korea. *It will never happen. China, unless pressured, will never crack down on what crosses Kim Jong Il's border.*

Six: Stress that a new resolution is needed for further action. *Which means stress the need for further inaction.*

We didn't need a UN resolution. We needed action. We should have taken out their nuke sites. We should have forced China to act with immediate tariffs. We should have struck immediately because, with every second that passed, we became more calcified.

The eyes of the world were on us. Eyes in Pyongyang. Eyes in Beijing. Eyes in Tehran. Those eyes saw weakness. We should be glad none of them struck us while we sat on our pathetic behinds and waited for sanctions to take effect.

We are still alive, so we still have time to learn the lesson. We can choose to be toothless herbivores, chewing our cud, waiting to be preyed upon. Or we can be carnivores, with the power to bare our fangs and to use them.

China

To the extent that we need to pressure North Korea, the issue is not North Korea alone. This is about China because North Korea would not exist without

China. North Korea is China's Junkyard Dog. China is responsible for 70 percent of North Korea's imports. They have leverage and they must be forced to use it.

We ought to impose massive tariffs on all Chinese goods coming into the United States and force China to call off their mad dog. Sanctions aren't enough. What's left to sanction in North Korea? We must be willing to give up the cheap shoes sent to us by the shipload from China.

Americans are more addicted to cheap goods from China than an addict was to the heroin that they exported a hundred years ago. We must be willing to give up the toys, the gadgets and the clothes—all the meaningless garbage that is heaped upon us by China and their American agents if we are to survive.

We also need to stop borrowing money from them unless we want to be sucked into their sphere of influence and allow them to become the world's super-power. As the Bible points out, the borrower is the slave to the lender. Our only alternative is to go deeper and deeper into a state of indentured servitude with those who are our enemy.

The South American Dictators

There is an amazing amount of ignorance regarding the Chavez nation of Venezuela. Most people don't know this, but this despicable despot has driven maybe half of the Jewish community out of Venezuela—according to the *Wall Street Journal*. Did you know anything about that? Unless you actually read the *Wall Street Journal*, you haven't heard anything about the politics of intimidation going on amongst Mr. Chavez's followers toward minorities—mainly Jews.

Did you know that in 1998, the year Hugo Chavez was elected president there were 22,000 Jews in Venezuela and that today the Jewish population is esti-mated at between 10,000-15,000? Chavez has said things that, if translated from the Spanish to the German, could have been spoken by Adolf Hitler himself.

Hugo Chavez has given anti-Semitism a new home.

But no one is paying any attention to this.

I wonder if Prime Minister Gordon Brown would invite Hugo Chavez to have tea with the Queen. I ask you these questions because it shows you which way the wind is blowing in England and it's not blowing in the direction of free-dom. It's blowing in the direction of fascism, my friend.

During the Cold War, Marxist governments sometimes worked with Islamic terrorists. There is every reason to think that this could happen again with the Hispanocommunists to the south of us. Here are some interesting examples straight from the *Wall Street Journal*:

- Graffiti, often bearing the signature of the Venezuelan Communist Party and its youth organization, have appeared on synagogues and Jewish buildings, with messages like "*mata niños*" ("child killers"), "*judios afuera*" ("Jews get out") and "*judios perros*" ("Jews are dogs"), and swastikas linked to stars of David by an equals sign.

- Sammy Eppel, a columnist for the independent Caracas newspaper *El Universal*, has documented hundreds of instances of anti-Semitism in government media. To take one particularly noxious example in September 2006. *El Diario de Caracas*, until recently one of the country's most important papers, published an editorial containing these fiery words: "Let us pay attention to the behavior of the Israeli-Zionist associations, unions, and federations that are conspiring in Venezuela to take control of our finances, our industries, commerce, construction–which are infiltrating our government and politics. Possibly we will have to expel them from our country . . . as other nations have done."

- Mario Silva, host of a popular pro-Chavez television show called "*La Hojilla*" ("The Razor Blade"), has repeatedly named prominent Venezuelan Jews as antigovernment conspirators and called on other Jews to denounce them. "Rabbi Jacobo Benzaquén and Rabbi Pynchas Brener are actively participating in the conspiracy in conjunction with the media," Silva has said. "So as not to be called an anti-Semite," he added, "I repeat that those Jewish businessmen not involved in the conspiracy should say so."

- Armed government agents have conducted two unannounced raids on the Hebraica club during the past five years. The first occurred during the early morning hours of Nov. 29, 2004, when two dozen men wearing masks invaded the elementary school just as pupils were arriving for class. In the second, which came shortly after midnight on Dec. 2, 2007, government agents broke through the front gate and disrupted hundreds of celebrants at a wedding party in the nearby synagogue. In each case, allegedly, the agents were looking for weapons and other evidence of "subversive activity."

- The last few years have seen the creation of a terrorist group in Venezuela calling itself Hezbollah in Latin America. The group has already claimed responsibility for placing two small bombs outside the American Embassy in Caracas in October 2006—one of them, it is thought, intended for the Embassy of Israel. Although neither of the two bombs detonated, the group's website hailed the man who planted them as a "brother mujahedin" and has urged other, simultaneous attacks throughout Venezuela in solidarity with Hezbollah in Lebanon.[4]

The threat that Chavez represents cannot be ignored. Giving Islamofascism a patron in this hemisphere could be extremely dangerous to the U.S. It is inexcusable that our politicians and our media have not spread more awareness of what is going on.

Great nations all have their great moments in history. For the Roman Empire, the *Pax Romana* was a time of relative peace and stability from 27 BC to 180 AD. Great Britain's *Pax Britannica* went from 1815 and the defeat of Napoleon until the beginning of World War One.

Our *Pax Americana* began in 1945, and some would argue that we are now in its final days. Though our economy is strong, and our military is the best in the world, our national will to live is failing. We have the money, but we send it to China. We have the troops, but we do not use them. We have borders, but we pretend they don't exist.

America is squandering its legacy. We stand on the shoulders of giants, the great men who built this nation–the generals, the scientists, the leaders. The

Pattons, the Saulks, the Roosevelts. But they are all gone, and no one has arisen to take their place. Today, our generals are detractors, not attackers. Our scientists are besmirchers, not researchers. And our leaders are men in traction, not men of action.

Who can put an end date on the *Pax Americana?* Will it come in 2010? Will it be the next Islamofascist attack? Or did it occur when we handed power over to the left? In any event, we have begun a new era. We are moving from the *Pax Americana* to the *Lax Americana*. The disease of liberalism has affected our nerve centers and is eating away at our ability to function. Only Savage surgery can save us from this self-inflicted illness.

The Home Front's Borders: The Ongoing Battle Against Amnesty

As I write this, Obama is attempting to change America forever by forcing on us an unworkable, impoverishing and unhealthy socialized medicine. But even in the middle of that fight he's not stopping. He has also made it abundantly clear that "comprehensive immigration reform" is next. I hope that healthcare teaches the Obama juggernaut that it is mortal like all the rest of humanity. I hope healthcare will stop Obama's "string of successes." If "healthcare reform" were stopped, that would not just help the sick and the healthy. It would also make it easier to stop his next agenda item. Amnesty for illegal aliens needs to be stopped!

Technically, Obama has already begun to officially work for a new amnesty bill. There can be no doubt it will be much worse than the one Bush tried to get passed. He met with a "bipartisan" group on June 25, 2009 to launch it. He announced, "reform that finally brings the 12 million people who are here illegally out of the shadows by requiring them to take steps to become legal citizens."[5] He wants an "effective way to recognize and legalize the status of undocumented workers that are here now."[6]

This is unbelievable! Obama's claim to want to protect the borders better is nonsense. When we allow illegals—who, by the way, broke our laws—to become citizens, we are rewarding that behavior. Amnesty sends a message to many more who are currently South of the border to come in. Eventually, they know, we'll give up and grant citizenship. We are saying to every foreigner who might want to sneak over here, *don't respect our laws; after all, we don't.*

True, we have a border that is hard to protect. Yes, we should do more to guard it. We should also do more to keep it from being crossed unlawfully. But nothing we do will matter if we don't also find and expel the illegals who manage to get over here.

We simply do not have the power to stop illegal immigration *only* at the border. We need to also expel them when they get past the border. If they know that we will do this, fewer will make the attempt. Giving them citizenship will mandate that we have many more illegal immigrants trying to cross.

It should surprise no one that Obama only allowed Republicans who already agreed with him to take part in his "bipartisan" meeting. Republican Congressman Steve King of Iowa, for example, was not invited. His office gave out a press release that said,

> The American people want this Administration to enforce existing immigration laws and secure our borders. A recent Washington Post-ABC News poll revealed that 74 percent of Americans believe the government is not doing enough to keep illegal immigrants from entering the country.
>
> The balance of the views inside the room at today's White House immigration summit does not reflect the views of the American public. Despite overwhelming opposition to amnesty within the U.S. House of Representatives, Congressman Lamar Smith of Texas will be the lone House Republican invited who opposes comprehensive amnesty. The White House stacked the deck and packed today's summit with amnesty advocates. President Obama wants an amnesty bill, and while cynically creating a false perception of inclusiveness and bipartisanship, brought in a group that, almost without exception, supports his vision of rewarding law breakers.

The mainstream media dutifully reported the Obama line that this meeting was bipartisan. Changing the make-up of the United States through high-speed, high-volume immigration is virtually the same as ending the United States. It will be like we were taken and transported to a half-foreign country without even being asked.

We conservatives must do our best to press for stronger borders, language, and culture. Our borders must be respected and our security preserved. Our language must be respected—it is the inheritance and identity of our nation. American culture is worth preserving.

Obama casually disallowed anyone who disagreed with him from having a voice in his decision-making. The media backed him up. That shows you what is happening in the whole American government. He and the Democrats will work to silence all dissenting views. Their slavish followers in the media will cover for them. We have already seen that the Democrats aren't satisfied with being a mere majority. They want to be the only voice in America.

The "bipartisan" efforts that Obama engages in are not attempts to work for a consensus. He picks the RINOs (Republicans In Name Only) who already agree with him and rewards them. He marginalizes Republicans who are still conservatives. His agenda is to remake the Republicans into Democrats. He wants to control political speech.

The reports from the Department of Homeland Security are another aspect of this same brutal attempt to control all speech. They show us a government intent on using their power to intimidate and marginalize the opposition.

Obama's liberal globalist friends overseas have started an experiment in one method of intimidation—using their borders.

We need to be on the lookout for what comes next, both here and over there.

Chapter Notes

[1] Charles McVety, "Michael Savage first American banned from Britain for defamation of Islam," *Jewish Times*, May 13, 2009, http://www.jewishtribune.ca /TribuneV2/index.php/200905131642/Michael-Savage-first-American-banned-from-Britain-for-defamation-of-Islam.html (Last viewed July 29, 2009).

[2] Ibid.

[3] Kevin Fagan, "Doctor killed in mysterious elevator shaft fall," *San Francisco Chronicle,* December 3, 2008. http://www.sfgate.com/cgibin/ article.cgi?f= /c/a/2008/12/03/MNVE14GCD6.DTL (Last viewed on July 29, 2009).

[4] Travis Pantin, "Hugo Chavez's Jewish Problem," *Wall Street Journal,* July 24, 2008, http://online.wsj.com/public/article_print/ SB121685054638578771.html (Last viewed on July 29, 2009).

[5] Robert L. Reeves, "Obama launches immigration reform," *Manila Bulletin,* July 11, 2009. http://www.mb.com.ph/articles/210363/obama-launches-immigration-reform (Last viewed July 29, 2009).

[6] Kate Riley, "Obama's practical immigration-reform approach: Legalize status of illegal workers," *Seattle Times*, July 2, 2009. http://seattletimes. nwsource.com/ html/opinion/2009413016_kate03.html (Last viewed July 29, 2009).

Epilogue
Now What?

As a matter of principle, we don't support such bans.
They tend to be selective, in that only popular speech is allowed
and unpopular speech is not allowed.[1]

–Ibrahim Hooper, Council of American-Islamic Relations

While some of these people may express views
that others find disagreeable, often the cure
(i.e. nations using "their borders as a weapon of censorship")
is worse than the disease.[2]

–Jameel Jaffer, an attorney for the American Civil Liberties Union

Free speech may become an endangered species in the Western World, even though the region was originally its native habitat. First it is me, but soon it will be others–unless this censorship is stopped.

It would be comforting if we could say that Great Britain was a country of no consequence. It would be wonderful if their "name and shame" list did not matter. After all, I wouldn't care if Iran announced that I was banned.

But Britain is a close ally of the United States. It is a Western nation with treaty obligations (shared by the U.S.) that demand free speech. Britain's ban has horrible implications for free speech in the Western World. This is even more urgent, because Americans were certainly involved in the ban. It is impossible to see any way British bureaucrats could have put my name on the list without the

171

help and even instigation from some person or groups in the United States. And it may even have involved our own government.

Free speech is at risk because powerful forces do not want to be criticized. We see this in the US. The Department of Homeland Security is issuing reports that intimidate opposing political speech. These reports associate conservatism with terrorism. The "Fairness Doctrine" may be imposed in order to cripple talk radio. The First Amendment is not being honored by the government.

You need to take action! Simply reading a book doesn't help the cause of free speech. Ideas need to be matched by deeds.

What can you do?

First, you can help me and the cause of free speech by writing to your Senator or Congressman on my behalf. Write a letter, print it out, put it in an envelope, put a stamp on it, and send it to Washington. You can easily look up the address for both your Senators and Congressman on the web. I ask you to write a letter to all of them.

As I pursue legal remedies and pursue more information about what has happened through Freedom of Information laws, I find that I have burdensome legal expenses. You can contribute to my legal defense fund by going to:

http://www.michaelsavage.wnd.com/?pageId=134

and hitting the donate button. It will allow you to use credit or debit cards. Or simply go to http://www.michaelsavage.com and follow the link to the page.

You can also send a check by mail to:

Michael Savage Legal Defense Fund
110 Pacific Avenue, Box 135
San Francisco, CA 94111

Another way to support me is to buy any books of mine you have not read. I have written a number of books about various issues that are important to our country. These books say what needs to be said about national security, religion and our nation's heritage, immigration, and other important matters. Go to my website and order for yourself, as well as for your friends and family.

You can also help me and the cause of free speech by spreading the word about what has happened to me. One way to do this would be to loan or give this book to a friend or co-worker. You can also buy more copies to give away.

Finally, while you are writing your Congressman about Michael Savage being banned from Britain, you should also consider the pressing issues that Congress and the Senate are considering right now. Sometimes the people can stop the rich and powerful! Congress voted against TARP the first time, despite immense corporate pressure from Wall Street. Also, listeners to talk radio defeated Bush's amnesty bill for illegal immigrants. We can win if we really commit ourselves to winning! Don't despair! Never give up!

Write a letter to Congress about health care. Write about the next amnesty bill Obama wants to pass. Write and tell your Senator and Representative what you want them to do. It can make a difference. If you don't take action, you will make no difference. Take action!

What will happen if I lose this battle? The governments on both sides of the Atlantic will be emboldened. Perhaps a victory of the Conservatives in Britain might change things, but in the United States, the Obama Administration will only continue to push for intimidation and the end of all opposing voices. The criminal justice system will be used to harass conservatives in the name of protecting against terrorism. The Fairness Doctrine or some equally damaging regulation will be used to destroy Talk Radio. Government control of the economy will give bureaucrats the power to unofficially punish anyone they don't like. If health care "reform" passes, the government will have new levels of knowledge about all your health issues and new ways to keep you in line.

Don't let this happen! We need to push back now; not later.

Take action!

The Weather Vein

I am Moses, Abraham, and Isaac
I am Charlemagne
I am John Wayne
I am Coltrane

They tried to suppress me
Tried to redress me
Called me incorrect
Deserving no respect

I am Patton... I am Hatton... even Mountbatten
I am Eisenhower... not a wallflower

I am Washington
I am Pershing
I'm MacArthur
I am Kipling
I'm Audie Murphy
I am Sky King

I am Huxley, Orwell, Russell
I am Pauling, not falling
I am Madame Curie and Louis Pasteur
I am the Bald Eagle

They'll steal your crown
Trample you down
Take your good name
Put it to shame

I am Gene Autry, Roy Rogers, Tom Mix
They tried to push me over the River Styx
But it won't mix with my true blood,
Which runs thick for America

I am the ban of those vain
I am the weather vein

Chapter Notes

1 "Britain's ban of Savage decried by detractors," *The San Francisco Chronicle*, May 6, 2009, http://www.sfgate.com/cgi-bin/article.cgi?f=/c/a/2009/05/05/MN3617FA8K.DTL (Last viewed on July 23, 2009).

2 Ibid.

Appendix I
Interview with John O'Sullivan

After the emails about the British Home Office's decision to ban me were made public in the *Daily Mail*, John O'Sullivan wrote a scathing and yet humorous piece for the *New York Post* entitled, "Condemned by Their Own Laptops." O'Sullivan is now the executive editor of Radio Free Europe/Radio Liberty in Prague. I interviewed him about his editorial on my show shortly after his article appeared.

Michael: John O'Sullivan, welcome to *The Savage Nation*.

John: Hi Michael. Thanks for having me on.

Michael: Great article! Because it's about me. But what made you write this all of a sudden?

John: When I saw the story, and particularly when I saw the emails from the officials in the Home Office, in which they gave their real reasons for keeping Michael Savage out of the country, I was reminded very strongly of a very well-known and world-wide popular British BBC television sitcom called *"Yes, Prime Minister."*

Yes, Prime Minister is a kind of British comic version of *The West Wing*. It describes the way government is really run. In other words, you have the civil servants who mastermind everything, and the poor old politicians are jerked about and made to look foolish. So you have this clever, manipulative, Machiavellian civil servant called Sir Humphrey, and you have a decent but feckless Prime

Minister called Jim Hacker. Jim loses about nine out of every ten battles he has with Sir Humphrey. The Prime Minister is manipulated again and again.

Sir Humphrey is a clever and crafty sort of fellow. The way those emails were written, reminded me of Sir Humphrey. Namely [engages in imaginary dialogue]:

"We have got to keep Michael Savage out of the country."

"Why is that? Is he a dangerous terrorist?"

*"No, no. The reason is that he's **not** a dangerous terrorist, because we need to have some people who aren't dangerous terrorists on the list in order to make it plain that we're not biased against dangerous terrorists. We've got too many of them on the ban list already."*

So this is such a kind of delicious absurdity that I thought, *Well I'll write a piece about this, pointing out that it is very similar to the comedy of* Yes, Prime Minister, *but that it has a somewhat serious side too.*

Michael: I think Sir Humphrey would never have put that in an email though.

John: Well, that's exactly right. One of the things I said was that if there was a real Sir Humphrey, one of the old school of mandarins, he would have known not to put things on paper. There's a famous remark by the Scotch Whiskey mandate Jimmy MacMillan: "Do right and fear no man. Don't write and fear no woman." Well, now it's not women you have to be afraid of. It's the front page of the *New York Times* or in this case the *Daily Mail*, a conservative paper, which has got a good record of getting its hands on confidential documents from within Labour governments and publishing to the world to the great embarrassment of the government.

Michael: This does not reflect well on Britain's "naming and shaming" practice.

John: Well, the idea behind this "naming and shaming" is very curious. Obviously, every now and then a government declares it doesn't want some people into the country. Technically they have become *persona non grata*. And I think every government has a right to keep out people who might be a danger to the people–to keep out foreigners who might be dangerous in one way or the other. But in this case they were looking around for people who weren't trying to come into the country–I gather you weren't trying to come into Britain.

Certainly they put on the list people who couldn't possibly come into the country, including two Russian skinheads who murdered people, who are serving long jail sentences in Russia, so that even if they wanted to enter Britain–and there is no evidence that they do–they would be allowed out of prison in Russia to do so. So why put these people on a list? Why publicize the list? Why embarrass some people by putting their names alongside others as dangerous characters?

And the answer to that question is that the government actually wanted to have people on the list who weren't terrorists and who weren't radical extreme Islamists because they had a group of these on the list and they thought if they published the list of people who really were dangerous–and almost all of them turned out to be radical, extremist Muslims–it would look as though they were anti-Islam.

So they looked around for people who might be plausibly attacked and they put them all together on a list and they then published the whole list saying, "Look, we're not biased against Islamist terrorists; we are keeping out other people who are dangerous." But, unfortunately for them, they put Michael Savage's name on the list.

So the purpose of this was very Machiavellian. It was an attempt to say, "Look, the world is full of dangerous people and we've made a random selection so there's nothing here that says that we are biased against any one group or another." However justified that intention might be, the idea of putting perfectly innocent people on a list with a lot of villains, and then saying, "We're keeping them all out," is obviously unjust to the innocent people.

And of course, in this case, it is producing a case of slander. And I would think that if the Home Secretary official responsible for this continues to fight that case, she–that is Jacquie Smith, a woman, our last Home Secretary–she would be humiliated in court. Because fundamentally these leaked emails suggest bad faith on the part of the British Government–as simple as that.

Michael: Do you think this is a characteristic of the British Government?

179

John: It is not characteristic of British Government, it seems to me, over the years, where standards of honesty and behavior are, you know, by standards of government, not bad. Pretty good. But there's recently been a huge scandal in Britain of a very similar kind.

Damian McBride, a Downing Street aid to Gordon Brown, the Prime Minister, was discovered sending scurrilous emails, in which he was trying to spread rumors about the sex lives of leading opposition politicians, leading Conservatives and their families–suggesting that the wife of one prominent Conservative had a shameful disease and that kind of thing.

Now, immediately after this happened he was disowned–well, you would expect that–and the Prime Minister said he was shocked and horrified that this had been going on. Again, you would expect that. But when you add these two cases together, you do get the impression that there is a culture of deceit and slander really at the heart of the British government at the moment.

I don't think it is a permanent thing and I don't think that it particularly comes from civil servants. I think it comes from the temporary civil servants brought in, the political loyalists around Labour ministers who are brought in. And I do think that standards of political morality in the generation of new Labour–political operatives who came in twelve years ago and who are still in government–I do think those moral standards are low. And they've begun to infect the Civil Service as well–the apolitical civil service.

I think anyone who has seen what has been happening in Britain in recent years has to be worried that the once high standard of political morality–and I don't necessarily know that you will agree with this–the once high standard of political morality has really declined seriously. And I think that should worry people in Britain and outside.

Michael: John O'Sullivan, thank you very much for your article!

John: Michael, thank you very much indeed. I very much enjoyed being on your show.

Appendix II

Petition to The United States Congress

PETITION FOR THE REMOVAL OF
BRITAIN'S BAN ON MICHAEL SAVAGE

To: Congress of The United States

Whereas, Michael Savage, with America's third largest radio talk-show audience, has been banned from Britain by Prime Minister Gordon Brown;

Whereas, Brown listed Savage's name alongside Russian skinheads imprisoned for murdering 10 immigrants and a Hamas terrorist who executed two Jewish parents and bashed in the head of their 4-year-old daughter;

Whereas, contrary to the accusations of the Prime Minister, Savage has never advocated violence and repeatedly has called for the lawful enforcement of America's borders, language and culture;

Whereas, freedom of speech must be protected to ensure the future of our democracy;

Whereas, Savage was honored with the Freedom of Speech Award by the radio industry in 2007;

Whereas, Savage's freedom has been denied, his health has suffered and his very life may be in danger because of the Prime Minister's actions;

SIGN THE PETITION

We, the undersigned, appeal to your good offices to act with the U.S. State Department and Secretary of State Hillary Clinton to persuade the British government to immediately remove Michael Savage's name from its list of banned murderers and terrorists.

_____

_____

_____

_____

_____

_____

_____

_____

_____

_____

_____

_____